DEPARTMENT OF THE NAVY
HEADQUARTERS UNITED STATES MARINE CORPS
3000 MARINE CORPS PENTAGON
WASHINGTON, DC 20350-3000

I0426285

OPERATIONS AND TACTICS INSTRUCTOR TRAINING AND READINESS MANUAL

DEPARTMENT OF THE NAVY
HEADQUARTERS UNITED STATES MARINE CORPS
3000 MARINE CORPS PENTAGON
WASHINGTON, DC 20350-3000

NAVMC 3500.36A
C 469
22 May 08

NAVMC 3500.36A

From: Commandant of the Marine Corps
To: Distribution List

Subj: OPERATIONS AND TACTICS INSTRUCTOR TRAINING AND READINESS MANUAL
      (SHORT TITLE: OTI T&R MANUAL)

Ref: (a) MCO P3500.72A
      (b) MCO 1553.3A
      (c) MCO 3400.3F
      (d) MCO 3500.27B W/Erratum
      (e) MCRP 3-0A
      (f) MCRP 3-0B
      (g) MCO 1553.2A

1. <u>Purpose</u>. In the Commandant's "The Way Forward" letter published in 2006, he established the requirement to develop a "Ground MAWTS." He acknowledged MSTP and MAWTS-1 success in preparing the Command and Aviation elements of the MAGTF for full spectrum conflict and stated that a similar capability for training must exist for the Ground element. In the summer of 2007, the Marine Corps Tactics & Operations Group (MCTOG) was activated to provide this capability. The Commandant highlighted the need for this new organization to standardize training and instructor qualifications. He envisioned MCTOG as an organization that would produce trainers of all ranks who could conduct detailed planning to integrate organic, MAGTF, Joint, and interagency assets into planning, training, and operations. Furthermore, he established the requirement for graduates of MCTOG to be able to plan and conduct MAGTF operations, integrate the six warfighting functions in training and operations, plan and execute kinetic and non-kinetic fires, and build mission training plans. As MAWTS has refined over the years a culture of training excellence and standardization for the ACE, MCTOG must "inculcate a unit training culture at all levels" within the GCE. Per reference (a), this T&R Manual establishes training standards, regulations, and practices to fulfill this training requirement. This NAVMC supersedes NAVMC 3500.36.

2. <u>Scope</u>

   a. The Core Capability Mission Essential Task (MET) in this manual is specifically used to provide focus for development of training standards for Operations Officers, Assistant Operations Officers, Operations Chiefs, Fire Support Coordinators, Fires Chiefs, and Marine Gunners. Per reference (g) MCTOG will develop formal instruction to provide a standardized course for the training and education of Marines in these billets.

   b. Per reference (b) commanders shall conduct an internal assessment of the unit's ability to execute each MET and prepare a definitive plan of attack to achieve MET proficiency by developing long-, mid-, and short-range training plans. Proficiency in OTI T&R Manual standards is critical to the success of any operational unit required to plan and conduct combat operations.

    c. Using this T&R Manual and other pertinent references, commanders will conduct evaluations (formal and informal) of their unit's ability to accomplish their METs. These training evaluations will be conducted at appropriate points in the unit's training cycle to determine MET proficiency and adjust training priorities.

    d. MCTOG will use references (a) thru (g) to ensure programs of instruction meet skill training requirements established in this manual.

3. Information. CG, TECOM will update this T&R Manual as necessary to provide current and relevant training standards to commanders. All questions pertaining to the Marine Corps Ground T&R Program and Unit Training Management should be directed to: Commanding General, TECOM (Ground Training Branch C 469), 1019 Elliot Road, Quantico, VA 22134.

4. Command. This Directive is applicable to the Marine Corps Total Force.

5. Certification. Reviewed and approved this date.

J. B. LASTER
By direction

Distribution: PCN 10033197300

    Copy to: 7000260 (2)
            8145001 (1)

2

LOCATOR SHEET

Subj: OPERATIONS AND TACTICS INSTRUCTOR TRAINING AND READINESS MANUAL,
       (SHORT TITLE: OTI T&R MANUAL)

Location: _____
               (Indicate location(s) of copy(ies) of this Manual.)

RECORD OF CHANGES

Log completed change action as indicated.

Change Number	Date of Change	Date Entered	Signature of Person Incorporated Change

OTI T&R MANUAL

TABLE OF CONTENTS

OTI T&R MANUAL

CHAPTER 1

OVERVIEW

OTI T&R MANUAL

CHAPTER 1

OVERVIEW

1000. INTRODUCTION

1. The T&R Program is the Marine Corps' primary tool for planning, conducting and evaluating training, and assessing training readiness. Subject Matter Experts (SMEs) from the operating forces developed core capability Mission Essential Task Lists (METLs) for ground communities derived from the Marine Corps Task List (MCTL). T&R Manuals are built around these METLs and all events contained in T&R Manuals relate directly to this METL. This comprehensive T&R Program will help to ensure the Marine Corps continues to improve its combat readiness by training more efficiently and effectively. Ultimately, this will enhance the Marine Corps' ability to accomplish real-world missions.

2. The T&R Manual contains the individual and collective training requirements to prepare units to accomplish their combat mission. The T&R Manual is not intended to be an encyclopedia that contains every minute detail of how to accomplish training. Instead, it identifies the minimum standards that Marines must be able to perform in combat. The T&R Manual is a fundamental tool for commanders to build and maintain unit combat readiness. Using this tool, leaders can construct and execute an effective training plan that supports the unit's METL. More detailed information on the Marine Corps Ground T&R Program is found in reference (a).

1001. UNIT TRAINING

1. The training of Marines to perform as an integrated unit in combat lies at the heart of the T&R program. Unit and individual readiness are directly related. Individual training and the mastery of individual core skills serve as the building blocks for unit combat readiness. A Marine's ability to perform critical skills required in combat is essential. However, it is not necessary to have all individuals within a unit fully trained in order for that organization to accomplish its assigned tasks. Manpower shortfalls, temporary assignments, leave, or other factors outside the commander's control, often affect the ability to conduct individual training. During these periods, unit readiness is enhanced if emphasis is placed on the individual training of Marines on-hand. Subsequently, these Marines will be mission ready and capable of executing as part of a team when the full complement of personnel is available.

2. Commanders will ensure that all tactical training is focused on their combat mission. The T&R Manual is a tool to help develop the unit's training plan. In most cases, unit training should focus on achieving unit proficiency in the core capabilities METL. However, commanders will adjust their training focus to support METLs associated with a major OPLAN/CONPLAN or named operation as designated by their higher commander and reported accordingly in the Defense Readiness Reporting System (DRRS). Tactical

training will support the METL in use by the commander and be tailored to
meet T&R standards. Commanders at all levels are responsible for effective
combat training. The conduct of training in a professional manner consistent
with Marine Corps standards cannot be over emphasized.

3. Commanders will provide personnel the opportunity to attend formal and
operational level courses of instruction as required by this Manual.
Attendance at all formal courses must enhance the warfighting capabilities of
the unit as determined by the unit commander.

1002. UNIT TRAINING MANAGEMENT

1. Unit Training Management (UTM) is the application of the Systems Approach
to Training (SAT) and the Marine Corps Training Principles. This is
accomplished in a manner that maximizes training results and focuses the
training priorities of the unit in preparation for the conduct of its wartime
mission.

2. UTM techniques, described in references (b) and (e), provide commanders
with the requisite tools and techniques to analyze, design, develop,
implement, and evaluate the training of their unit. The Marine Corps
Training Principles, explained in reference (b), provide sound and proven
direction and are flexible enough to accommodate the demands of local
conditions. These principles are not inclusive, nor do they guarantee
success. They are guides that commanders can use to manage unit-training
programs. The Marine Corps training principles are:

    - Train as you fight
    - Make commanders responsible for training
    - Use standards-based training
    - Use performance-oriented training
    - Use mission-oriented training
    - Train the MAGTF to fight as a combined arms team
    - Train to sustain proficiency
    - Train to challenge

3. To maintain an efficient and effective training program, leaders at every
level must understand and implement UTM. Guidance for UTM and the process
for establishing effective programs are contained in references (a) through
(g).

1003. SUSTAINMENT AND EVALUATION OF TRAINING

1. The evaluation of training is necessary to properly prepare Marines for
combat. Evaluations are either formal or informal, and performed by members
of the unit (internal evaluation) or from an external command (external
evaluation).

2. Marines are expected to maintain proficiency in the training events for
their MOS at the appropriate grade or billet to which assigned. Leaders are
responsible for recording the training achievements of their Marines.
Whether it involves individual or collective training events, they must
ensure proficiency is sustained by requiring retraining of each event at or

before expiration of the designated sustainment interval. Performance of the training event, however, is not sufficient to ensure combat readiness. Leaders at all levels must evaluate the performance of their Marines and the unit as they complete training events, and only record successful accomplishment of training based upon the evaluation. The goal of evaluation is to ensure that correct methods are employed to achieve the desired standard, or the Marines understand how they need to improve in order to attain the standard. Leaders must determine whether credit for completing a training event is recorded if the standard was not achieved. While successful accomplishment is desired, debriefing of errors can result in successful learning that will allow ethical recording of training event completion. Evaluation is a continuous process that is integral to training management and is conducted by leaders at every level and during all phases of planning and the conduct of training. To ensure training is efficient and effective, evaluation is an integral part of the training plan. Ultimately, leaders remain responsible for determining if the training was effective.

3. The purpose of informal and formal evaluation is to provide commanders with a process to determine a unit's/Marine's proficiency in the tasks that must be performed in combat. Informal evaluations are conducted during every training evolution. Formal evaluations are often scenario-based, focused on the unit's METs, based on collective training standards, and usually conducted during higher-level collective events. References (a) and (f) provide further guidance on the conduct of informal and formal evaluations using the Marine Corps Ground T&R Program.

1004. ORGANIZATION

1. T&R Manuals are organized in one of two methods: unit-based or community-based. Unit-based T&R Manuals are written to support a type of unit (Infantry, Artillery, Tanks, etc.) and contain both collective and individual training standards. Community-based are written to support an Occupational Field, a group of related Military Occupational Specialties (MOSs), or billets within an organization (EOD, NBC, Intel, etc.), and usually only contain individual training standards. T&R Manuals are comprised of chapters that contain unit METs, collective training standards (CTS), and individual training standards (ITS) for each MOS, billet, etc.

2. The OTI T&R Manual is a community-based manual comprised of three (3) chapters. Because it is a community-based manual, not all the information contained in the Chapter 1 Overview is relevant to the application of the training standards in this manual. Combat Readiness Percentage for example, is not relevant to individual T&R events. Chapter 1 amplifies general information contained in reference (a). Chapter 2 lists the Core Capability MET and the related Operations Tactics Instructor (OTI) events. Chapter 3 contains OTI Individual Events complete with conditions, standards, and performance steps. Appendix A contains the Functional Area Matrix which defines the scope of each functional area. Appendix B is a Glossary of Terms which will assist the user in defining unique T&R terminology and some standard training related terms.

1005. T&R EVENT CODING

1. T&R events are coded for ease of reference. Each event has up-to a 4-4-4 digit identifier. The first up-to four digits are referred to as a "community" and represent the unit type or occupation (OTIC). The second up-to four digits represent the functional or duty area (PLAN, OPS, TRNG). The last four digits represent the level and sequence of the event.

2. The T&R levels are illustrated in Figure 1. An example of the T&R coding used in this Manual is shown in Figure 2.

Figure 1: T&R Event Levels

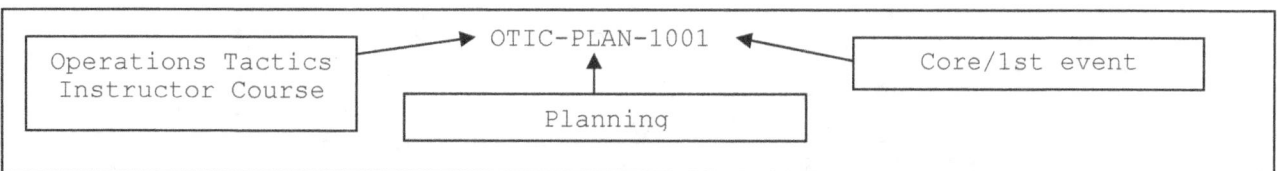

Figure 2: T&R Event Coding

1006. COMBAT READINESS PERCENTAGE

1. The Marine Corps Ground T&R Program includes processes to assess readiness of units and individual Marines. Every unit in the Marine Corps maintains a basic level of readiness based on the training and experience of the Marines in the unit. Even units that never trained together are capable of accomplishing some portion of their missions. Combat readiness assessment does not associate a quantitative value for this baseline of readiness, but uses a "Combat Readiness Percentage", as a method to provide a concise descriptor of the recent training accomplishments of units and Marines.

2. Combat Readiness Percentage (CRP) is the percentage of required training events that a unit or Marine accomplishes within specified sustainment intervals.

3. In unit-based T&R Manuals, unit combat readiness is assessed as a percentage of the successfully completed and current (within sustainment interval) key training events called "Evaluation-Coded" (E-Coded) Events. E-Coded Events and unit CRP calculation are described in follow-on paragraphs. CRP achieved through the completion of E-Coded Events is directly relevant to readiness assessment in DRRS.

4. Individual combat readiness, in both unit-based and community-based T&R Manuals, is assessed as the percentage of required individual events in which a Marine is current. This translates as the percentage of training events for his/her MOS and grade (or billet) that the Marine successfully completes within the directed sustainment interval. Individual skills are developed through a combination of 1000-level training (entry-level formal school courses), individual on-the-job training in 2000-level events, and follow-on formal school training. Skill proficiency is maintained by retraining in each event per the specified sustainment interval.

1007. EVALUATION-CODED (E-CODED) EVENTS

1. Unit-type T&R Manuals can contain numerous unit events, some for the whole unit and others for integral parts that serve as building blocks for training. To simplify training management and readiness assessment, only collective events that are critical components of a mission essential task (MET), or key indicators of a unit's readiness, are used to generate CRP for a MET. These critical or key events are designated in the T&R Manual as Evaluation-Coded (E-Coded) events. Formal evaluation of unit performance in these events is recommended because of their value in assessing combat readiness. Only E-Coded events are used to calculate CRP for each MET.

2. The use of a METL-based training program allows the commander discretion in training. This makes the T&R Manual a training tool rather than a prescriptive checklist.

1008. CRP CALCULATION

1. Collective training begins at the 3000 level (team, crew or equivalent). Unit training plans are designed to accomplish the events that support the unit METL while simultaneously sustaining proficiency in individual core skills. Using the battalion-based (unit) model, the battalion (7000-level) has collective events that directly support a MET on the METL. These collective events are E-Coded and the only events that contribute to unit CRP. This is done to assist commanders in prioritizing the training toward the METL, taking into account resource, time, and personnel constraints.

2. Unit CRP increases after the completion of E-Coded events. The number of E-Coded events for the MET determines the value of each E-Coded event. For example, if there are 4 E-Coded events for a MET, each is worth 25% of MET CRP. MET CRP is calculated by adding the percentage of each completed and current (within sustainment interval) E-Coded training event. The percentage for each MET is calculated the same way and all are added together and divided by the number of METS to determine unit CRP. For ease of calculation, we will say that each MET has 4 E-Coded events, each contributing 25% towards the completion of the MET. If the unit has

completed and is current on three of the four E-Coded events for a given MET, then they have completed 75% of the MET. The CRP for each MET is added together and divided by the number of METS to get unit CRP; unit CRP is the average of MET CRP.

For Example:

    MET 1: 75% complete   (3 of 4 E-Coded events trained)
    MET 2: 100% complete (6 of 6 E-Coded events trained)
    MET 3: 25% complete   (1 of 4 E-Coded events trained)
    MET 4: 50% complete   (2 of 4 E-Coded events trained)
    MET 5: 75% complete   (3 of 4 E-Coded events trained)

To get unit CRP, simply add the CRP for each MET and divide by the number of METS:

    MET CRP: 75 + 100 + 25 + 50 + 75 = 325

    Unit CRP: 325 (total MET CRP)/ 5 (total number of METS) = 65%

1009. T&R EVENT COMPOSITION

1. This section explains each of the components of a T&R event. These items are included in all events in each T&R manual.

    a. Event Code (see Sect 1006). The event code is a 4-4-4 character set. For individual training events, the first 4 characters indicate the occupational function or special skill. The second 4 characters indicate functional area (PLAN, OPS, TRNG). The third 4 characters are simply a numerical designator for the event.

    b. Event Title. The event title is the name of the event.

    c. E-Coded. This is a "yes/no" category to indicate whether or not the event is E-Coded. If yes, the event contributes toward the CRP of the associated MET. The value of each E-Coded event is based on number of E-Coded events for that MET. Refer to paragraph 1008 for detailed explanation of E-Coded events.

    d. Supported MET(s). List all METs that are supported by the training event.

    e. Sustainment Interval. This is the period, expressed in number of months, between evaluation or retraining requirements. Skills and capabilities acquired through the accomplishment of training events are refreshed at pre-determined intervals. It is essential that these intervals are adhered to in order to ensure Marines maintain proficiency.

    f. Billet. Individual training events may contain a list of billets within the community that are responsible for performing that event. This ensures that the billet's expected tasks are clearly articulated and a Marine's readiness to perform in that billet is measured.

g. <u>Grade</u>. Each individual training event will list the rank(s) at which Marines are required to learn and sustain the training event.

h. <u>Initial Training Setting</u>. For Individual T&R Events only, this specifies the location for initial instruction of the training event in one of three categories (formal school, managed on-the-job training, distance learning). Regardless of the specified Initial Training Setting, any T&R event may be introduced and evaluated during managed on-the-job training.

(1) "FORMAL" - When the Initial Training Setting of an event is identified as "FORMAL" (formal school), the appropriate formal school or training detachment is required to provide initial training in the event. Conversely, formal schools and training detachments are not authorized to provide training in events designated as Initial Training Setting "MOJT" or "DL." Since the duration of formal school training must be constrained to optimize Operating Forces' manning, this element provides the mechanism for Operating Forces' prioritization of training requirements for both entry-level (1000-level) and career-level (2000-level) T&R Events. For formal schools and training detachments, this element defines the requirements for content of courses.

(2) "DL" - Identifies the training event as a candidate for initial training via a Distance Learning product (correspondence course or MarineNet course).

(3) "MOJT" - Events specified for Managed On-the-Job Training are to be introduced to Marines, and evaluated, as part of training within a unit by supervisory personnel.

i. <u>Event Description</u>. Provide a description of the event purpose, objectives, goals, and requirements. It is a general description of an action requiring learned skills and knowledge (e.g. Camouflage the M1A1 Tank).

j. <u>Condition</u>. Describe the condition(s), under which tasks are performed. Conditions are based on a "real world" operational environment. They indicate what is provided (equipment, materials, manuals, aids, etc.), environmental constraints, conditions under which the task is performed, and any specific cues or indicators to which the performer must respond. When resources or safety requirements limit the conditions, this is stated.

k. <u>Standard</u>. The standard indicates the basis for judging effectiveness of the performance. It consists of a carefully worded statement that identifies the proficiency level expected when the task is performed. The standard provides the minimum acceptable performance parameters and is strictly adhered to. The standard for collective events is general, describing the desired end-state or purpose of the event. While the standard for individual events specifically describe to what proficiency level in terms of accuracy, speed, sequencing, quality of performance, adherence to procedural guidelines, etc., the event is accomplished.

l. <u>Event Components</u>. Describe the actions composing the event and help the user determine what must be accomplished and to properly plan for the event.

m. <u>Prerequisite Events</u>. Prerequisites are academic training or other T&R events that must be completed prior to attempting the task. They are lower-level events or tasks that give the individual/unit the skills required to accomplish the event. They can also be planning steps, administrative requirements, or specific parameters that build toward mission accomplishment.

n. <u>Chained Events</u>. Collective T&R events are supported by lower-level collective and individual T&R events. This enables unit leaders to effectively identify subordinate T&R events that ultimately support specific mission essential tasks. When the accomplishment of any upper-level events, by their nature, result in the performance of certain subordinate and related events, the events are "chained." The completion of chained events will update sustainment interval credit (and CRP for E-Coded events) for the related subordinate level events.

o. <u>Related Events</u>. Provide a list of all Individual Training Standards that support the event.

p. <u>References</u>. The training references are utilized to determine task performance steps, grading criteria, and ensure standardization of training procedures. They assist the trainee in satisfying the performance standards, or the trainer in evaluating the effectiveness of task completion. References are also important to the development of detailed training plans.

q. <u>Distance Learning Products</u> (IMI, CBT, MCI, etc.). Include this component when the event can be taught via one of these media methods vice attending a formal course of instruction or receiving MOJT.

r. <u>Support Requirements</u>. This is a list of the external and internal support the unit and Marines will need to complete the event. The list includes, but is not limited to:

- Range(s)/Training Area
- Ordnance
- Equipment
- Materials
- Other Units/Personnel
- Other Support Requirements

s. <u>Miscellaneous</u>. Provide any additional information that assists in the planning and execution of the event. Miscellaneous information may include, but is not limited to:

- Admin Instructions
- Special Personnel Certifications
- Equipment Operating Hours
- Road Miles

2. Community-based T&R manuals have several additional components not found in unit-based T&R manuals. These additions do not apply to this T&R Manual.

1010. CBRNE TRAINING

1. All personnel assigned to the operating force must be trained in chemical, biological, radiological, nuclear, and explosive incident defense (CBRNE), in order to survive and continue their mission in this environment. Individual proficiency standards are defined as survival and basic operating standards. Survival standards are those that the individual must master in order to survive CBRNE attacks. Basic operating standards are those that the individual, and collectively the unit, must perform to continue operations in a CBRNE environment.

2. In order to develop and maintain the ability to operate in an CBRNE environment, CBRNE training is an integral part of the training plan and events in this T&R Manual. Units should train under CBRNE conditions whenever possible. Per reference (c), all units must be capable of accomplishing their assigned mission in a contaminated environment.

1011. NIGHT TRAINING

1. While it is understood that all personnel and units of the operating force are capable of performing their assigned mission in "every climate and place," current doctrine emphasizes the requirement to perform assigned missions at night and during periods of limited visibility. Basic skills are significantly more difficult when visibility is limited.

2. To ensure units are capable of accomplishing their mission they must train under the conditions of limited visibility. Units should strive to conduct all events in this T&R Manual during both day and night/limited visibility conditions. When there is limited training time available, night training should take precedence over daylight training, contingent on individual, crew, and unit proficiency.

1012. OPERATIONAL RISK MANAGEMENT (ORM)

1. ORM is a process that enables commanders to plan for and minimize risk while still accomplishing the mission. It is a decision making tool used by Marines at all levels to increase operational effectiveness by anticipating hazards and reducing the potential for loss, thereby increasing the probability of a successful mission. ORM minimizes risks to acceptable levels, commensurate with mission accomplishment.

2. Commanders, leaders, maintainers, planners, and schedulers will integrate risk assessment in the decision-making process and implement hazard controls to reduce risk to acceptable levels. Applying the ORM process will reduce mishaps, lower costs, and provide for more efficient use of resources. ORM assists the commander in conserving lives and resources and avoiding unnecessary risk, making an informed decision to implement a course of action (COA), identifying feasible and effective control measures where specific measures do not exist, and providing reasonable alternatives for mission accomplishment. Most importantly, ORM assists the commander in determining the balance between training realism and unnecessary risks in training, the impact of training operations on the environment, and the adjustment of training plans to fit the level of proficiency and experience of

Sailors/Marines and leaders. Further guidance for ORM is found in references (b) and (d).

1013. APPLICATION OF SIMULATION

1. Simulations/Simulators and other training devices shall be used when they are capable of effectively and economically supplementing training on the identified training task. Particular emphasis shall be placed on simulators that provide training that might be limited by safety considerations or constraints on training space, time, or other resources. When deciding on simulation issues, the primary consideration shall be improving the quality of training and consequently the state of readiness. Potential savings in operating and support costs normally shall be an important secondary consideration.

2. Each training event contains information relating to the applicability of simulation. If simulator training applies to the event, then the applicable simulator(s) is/are listed in the "Simulation" section and the CRP for simulation training is given. This simulation training can either be used in place of live training, at the reduced CRP indicated; or can be used as a precursor training for the live event, i.e., weapons simulators, convoy trainers, observed fire trainers, etc. It is recommended that tasks be performed by simulation prior to being performed in a live-fire environment. However, in the case where simulation is used as a precursor for the live event, then the unit will receive credit for the live event CRP only. If a tactical situation develops that precludes performing the live event, the unit would then receive credit for the simulation CRP.

1014. MARINE CORPS GROUND T&R PROGRAM

1. The Marine Corps Ground T&R Program continues to evolve. The vision for Ground T&R Program is to publish a T&R Manual for every readiness-reporting unit so that core capability METs are clearly defined with supporting collective training standards, and to publish community-based T&R Manuals for all occupational fields whose personnel augment other units to increase their combat and/or logistic capabilities. The vision for this program includes plans to provide a Marine Corps Training Management Information System that enables tracking of unit and individual training accomplishments by unit commanders and small unit leaders, automatically computing CRP for both units and individual Marines based upon MOS and rank (or billet). Linkage of T&R Events to the Marine Corps Task List (MCTL), through the core capability METs, has enabled objective assessment of training readiness in the DRRS.

2. DRRS measures and reports on the readiness of military forces and the supporting infrastructure to meet missions and goals assigned by the Secretary of Defense. With unit CRP based on the unit's training toward its METs, the CRP will provide a more accurate picture of a unit's readiness. This will give fidelity to future funding requests and factor into the allocation of resources. Additionally, the Ground T&R Program will help to ensure training remains focused on mission accomplishment and that training readiness reporting is tied to units' METLs.

OTI T&R MANUAL

CHAPTER 2

MISSION ESSENTIAL TASKS MATRIX

OTI T&R MANUAL

CHAPTER 2

MISSION ESSENTIAL TASKS MATRIX

2000. OTI MISSION ESSENTIAL TASKS. The list below is the OTI Mission Essential Task List (METL). All METs for the OTI T&R are derived from the Marine Corps Task List (MCTL). They were selected specifically to represent the combat multiplier available to the Ground Combat Element (GCE) commanders at the battalion and regimental levels via the OTI. They allow the commander, through the operations officer, to drive operations across the GCE and are the basis of all instruction provided by MCTOG. Included in the matrix are the supporting events for each MET.

> MET 1: MCT 5.2 Prepare Plans and Orders
> MET 2: MCT 4.7 Train Forces and Personnel
> MET 3: MCT 1.6 Dominate the Area of Operations

2001. OTI MISSION ESSENTIAL TASK MATRIX

MET 1 - MCT 5.2 Prepare Plans and Orders	
OTIC-PLAN-2001	Direct the Marine Corps Planning Process
OTIC-PLAN-2002	Integrate intelligence into ground combat operations
OTIC-PLAN-2003	Integrate maneuver into ground combat operations
OTIC-PLAN-2004	Integrate supporting arms into ground combat operations
OTIC-PLAN-2005	Integrate information operations into ground combat operations
OTIC-PLAN-2006	Integrate civil military operations into ground combat operations
OTIC-PLAN-2007	Integrate logistics into ground combat operations
OTIC-PLAN-2008	Integrate communications into ground combat operations
OTIC-PLAN-2009	Integrate force protection into ground combat operations
OTIC-PLAN-2010	Integrate MAGTF support into ground combat operations
OTIC-PLAN-2011	Integrate joint, interagency, and coalition support into ground combat operations
OTIC-PLAN-2012	Develop an information management plan
OTIC-PLAN-2101	Participate in the Marine Corps Planning Process

MET 2 - MCT 4.7 Train Forces and Personnel	
OTIC-TRNG-2001	Manage unit training
OTIC-TRNG-2002	Conduct training
OTIC-TRNG-2003	Prepare a unit for combat
OTIC-TRNG-2004	Establish information management training requirements
OTIC-TRNG-2201	Design a training program
OTIC-TRNG-2202	Integrate GCE weapons capabilities into training programs
OTIC-TRNG-2203	Integrate threat weapons capabilities into training programs

MET 3 - MCT 1.6 Dominate the Area of Operations	
OTIC-OPS-2001	Establish a Command Post
OTIC-OPS-2002	Implement the orders process
OTIC-OPS-2003	Exercise command and control during ground combat operations
OTIC-OPS-2004	Integrate and synchronize the intelligence effort to support combat operations
OTIC-OPS-2005	Execute the information management plan
OTIC-OPS-2006	Execute duties of Fire Support Coordinator
OTIC-OPS-2101	Execute duties of Operations Chief
OTIC-OPS-2102	Execute duties of Fires Chief

OTI T&R MANUAL

CHAPTER 3

INDIVIDUAL EVENTS

CHAPTER 3

INDIVIDUAL EVENTS

3000. PURPOSE. This chapter details the individual events that pertain to the Operations and Tactics Instructor. These events are linked to a service-level Mission Essential Tasks (MET). This linkage tailor's individual training for the selected MET. Each individual event provides an event title, along with the conditions events will be performed under, and the standard to which the event must be performed to be successful.

3001. ADMINISTRATIVE NOTES. T&R events are coded for ease of reference. Each event has a 4-4-4 digit identifier. The first four digits represent the occupational field, military occupational field, or community (OTIC). The second four digits represent the functional or duty area. The last four digits represent the level, and identifier number of the event. Every individual event has an identifier number from 001 to 999.

3002. THE OPERATIONS AND TACTICS INSTRUCTOR. Graduates of MCTOG's resident Operations and Tactics Instructor Course (OTIC) receive a school code designating them as Operations and Tactics Instructors (OTI). The OTI graduate returns to his unit and becomes the conduit through which the OTTP facilitates the advanced and standardized training and preparation of the GCE unit for combat. In effect, the OTI, through the application of the OTTP, is the critical mechanism in establishing a dynamic, timely, and responsive GCE community of practice. The OTI becomes a training and combat multiplier through the application of skill sets established in this T&R. All events in this chapter are 2000-level "core-plus" events and represent the benchmark standards for operational planning.

3003. INDEX OF INDIVIDUAL EVENTS BY FUNCTIONAL AREA

EVENT	TITLE	PAGE
	PLANNING	
OTIC-PLAN-2001	Direct the Marine Corps Planning Process	3-4
OTIC-PLAN-2002	Integrate intelligence into ground combat operations	3-4
OTIC-PLAN-2003	Integrate maneuver into ground combat operations	3-6
OTIC-PLAN-2004	Integrate supporting arms into ground combat operations	3-7
OTIC-PLAN-2005	Integrate information operations into ground combat operations	3-8
OTIC-PLAN-2006	Integrate civil military operations into ground combat operations	3-9
OTIC-PLAN-2007	Integrate logistics into ground combat operations	3-10
OTIC-PLAN-2008	Integrate communications into ground combat operations	3-11
OTIC-PLAN-2009	Integrate force protection into ground combat operations	3-12
OTIC-PLAN-2010	Integrate MAGTF support into ground combat operations	3-13
OTIC-PLAN-2011	Integrate joint, interagency, and coalition support into ground combat operations	3-14
OTIC-PLAN-2012	Develop an information management plan.	3-15
OTIC-PLAN-2101	Participate in the Marine Corps Planning Process	3-16
	TRAINING	
OTIC-TRNG-2001	Manage unit training	3-16
OTIC-TRNG-2002	Conduct training	3-17
OTIC-TRNG-2003	Prepare a unit for combat	3-18
OTIC-TRNG-2004	Establish information management training requirements	3-19
OTIC-TRNG-2201	Design a training program	3-20
OTIC-TRNG-2202	Integrate GCE weapons capabilities into training programs	3-21
OTIC-TRNG-2203	Integrate threat weapons capabilities into training programs	3-21
	OPERATIONS	
OTIC-OPS-2001	Establish a Command Post	3-22
OTIC-OPS-2002	Implement the orders process	3-23
OTIC-OPS-2003	Exercise command and control during ground combat operations	3-24
OTIC-OPS-2004	Integrate and synchronize the intelligence effort to support combat operations	3-25
OTIC-OPS-2005	Execute the information management plan	3-26
OTIC-OPS-2006	Execute duties of Fire Support Coordinator	3-26
OTIC-OPS-2101	Execute duties of Operations Chief	3-28
OTIC-OPS-2102	Execute duties of Fires Chief	3-29

3004. INDIVIDUAL EVENTS

OTIC-PLAN-2001: Direct the Marine Corps Planning Process

EVALUATION-CODED: NO   **SUSTAINMENT INTERVAL:** 6 months

MOS PERFORMING: 0203, 0302, 0303, 0306, 0802, 1302, 1802, 1803

BILLETS: Operations Officer, Assistant Operations Officer, Fire Support Coordinator, Marine Gunner

GRADES: CWO-2, CWO-3, CWO-4, CAPT, MAJ, LTCOL

INITIAL TRAINING SETTING: FORMAL

CONDITION: Given a battalion task force or regimental combat team operating within a MAGTF/Joint/Combined/Interagency environment, higher headquarters' order, commander's guidance and references, while implementing the orders process.

STANDARD: Produce plans and orders which support the accomplishment of the mission and commander's intent.

PERFORMANCE STEPS:
1. Conduct mission analysis.
2. Convene and integrate a Red Cell into planning.
3. Develop courses of action.
4. Wargame courses of action.
5. Compare and recommend courses of action.
6. Develop appropriate staff products, operations plans, orders, annexes, and appendices.
7. Execute transition.

REFERENCES:
1. MCWP 3-40.1 Marine Air-Ground Task Force Command and Control
2. MCWP 5-1 Marine Corps Planning Process

MISCELLANEOUS:

ADMINISTRATIVE INSTRUCTIONS:

1. Performance steps are derived from task 0502-PLAN-1016. See MAGTF Plans Officer T&R Manual for additional information.
2. Estimates of supportability should be incorporated before COA decision determination.

OTIC-PLAN-2002: Integrate intelligence into ground combat operations

EVALUATION-CODED: NO   **SUSTAINMENT INTERVAL:** 6 months

MOS PERFORMING: 0203, 0302, 0303, 0306, 0313, 0321, 0369, 0802, 0848, 0861, 1302, 1371, 1802, 1803, 1812, 1833, 8007

BILLETS: Assistant Operations Officer, Fire Support Coordinator, Fires Chief, Gunner, Operations Chief, Operations Officer, Assistant Operations Chief

GRADES: GYSGT, MSGT, MGYSGT, CWO-2, CWO-3, CWO-4, CAPT, MAJ, LTCOL

INITIAL TRAINING SETTING: FORMAL

CONDITION: Given a battalion task force or regimental combat team operating within a MAGTF/Joint/Combined/Interagency environment, higher headquarters' operations order, commander's guidance and references, in conjunction with the intelligence section while implementing the orders process.

STANDARD: The commander is able to make informed decisions to conduct effective unit operations.

PERFORMANCE STEPS:
1. Identify the operational environment.
2. Identify and assess threat capabilities and intentions.
3. Identify desired methods, media, and products to support Intelligence Preparation of the Operational Environment.
4. Identify desired methods, media, and products to support the intelligence effort to the Marine Corps Planning Process.
5. Identify parameters and requirements to support intelligence estimates/assumptions.
6. Develop and recommend FFIRs/PIRs.
7. Integrate intelligence products into orders.
8. Identify desired methods, media, and products to support the intelligence effort during targeting.
9. Coordinate and integrate collection & ISR plans in support of operational design.

REFERENCES:
1. JP 2-01 Joint and National Intelligence Support to Military Operations
2. MCDP 1-0 Marine Corps Operations
3. MCRP 2-3A Intelligence Preparation of the Battlefield
4. MCWP 2-3 MAGTF Intelligence Production and Analysis
5. MCWP 2-6 Counterintelligence
6. MCWP 5-1 Marine Corps Planning Process
7. MSTP Pamphlet 2-0.1 The Red Cell

MISCELLANEOUS:

ADMINISTRATIVE INSTRUCTIONS: Performance steps are derived from tasks 0202-PLAN-1041, 0202-PLAN-1042, 0202-PLAN-1043, 0202-PLAN-1044, 0202-PLAN-1045, 0202-PLAN-1940, 0202-TRGT-1050, 0202-ANYS-1901, 0202-ANYS-1902, 0203-PLAN-1050, 0203-PLAN-1051, 0203-PLAN-1052, 0203-PLAN-1053, 0203-PLAN-1054, 0203-PLAN-1055, and 0203-TRGT-1060. See Intelligence T&R Manual for additional information.

OTIC-PLAN-2003: Integrate maneuver into ground combat operations

EVALUATION-CODED: NO   **SUSTAINMENT INTERVAL:** 6 months

MOS PERFORMING: 0203, 0302, 0303, 0306, 0313, 0321, 0369, 0802, 0848, 0861, 1302, 1371, 1802, 1803, 1812, 1833, 8007

BILLETS: Assistant Operations Officer, Fire Support Coordinator, Fires Chief, Gunner, Operations Chief, Operations Officer, Assistant Operations Chief

GRADES: GYSGT, MSGT, MGYSGT, CWO-2, CWO-3, CWO-4, CAPT, MAJ, LTCOL

INITIAL TRAINING SETTING: FORMAL

CONDITION: Given a battalion task force or regimental combat team operating within a MAGTF/Joint/Combined/Interagency environment, higher headquarters' operations order, commander's guidance and references, while implementing the orders process.

STANDARD: Develop a concept of operations and scheme of maneuver which employs combined arms to gain a position of advantage over the enemy in accordance with the mission and commander's intent.

PERFORMANCE STEPS:
1. Assess enemy center of gravity and critical vulnerabilities.
2. Determine decisive points.
3. Determine objectives.
4. Determine lines of operation.
5. Identify assets available.
6. Conduct a relative combat power assessment.
7. Determine type of operation to be conducted.
8. Determine forms of maneuver.
9. Determine scheme of maneuver which accomplishes the commander's intent.
10. Determine main and supporting efforts.
11. Coordinate external support.
12. Integrate GCE assets.
13. Task organize the force.
14. Organize the battlespace.
15. Establish control measures.
16. Integrate and synchronize warfighting functions.

REFERENCES:
1. MCDP 1-0 Marine Corps Operations
2. MCWP 3-1 Ground Combat Operations
3. MCDP 1-3 Tactics
4. MCWP 3-33.5 Counterinsurgency
5. MCWP 3-11.14 Helicopterborne Operations
6. MCWP 3-12 Marine Corps Tank Employment
7. MCWP 3-13 Employment of AAVs
8. MCWP 3-15 MAGTF Anti-Armor Operations
9. MCWP 3-16 Fire Support Coordination in the GCE
10. MCWP 3-17.1 River Crossing Operations
11. MCWP 3-17.3 MAGTF Breaching Operations
12. MCWP 3-31.5 Ship to Shore Movement

13. MCWP 3-32 Maritime Prepositioning Operations
14. MCWP 3-33.5 Military Operations In Urban Terrain
15. MCRP 3-11.1a Commander's Tactical Handbook
16. MCRP 5-12a Operational Terms & Graphics
17. FM 3-90 Tactics, 2001
18. FM 3-90.2 The Tank and Mechanized Infantry Battalion Task Force, 2003
19. TRADOC Pamphlet 525-3-2 Tactical Maneuver
20. MCRP 3-16.6 Multiservice Procedures for the Joint Application of
    Firepower (J-Fire)

OTIC-PLAN-2004: Integrate supporting arms into ground combat operations

EVALUATION-CODED: NO   **SUSTAINMENT INTERVAL**: 6 months

MOS PERFORMING: 0203, 0302, 0303, 0306, 0313, 0321, 0369, 0802, 0848, 0861, 1302, 1371, 1802, 1803, 1812, 1833

BILLETS: Assistant Operations Officer, Fire Support Coordinator, Fires Chief, Gunner, Operations Chief, Operations Officer, Assistant Operations Chief

GRADES: GYSGT, MSGT, MGYSGT, CWO-2, CWO-3, CWO-4, CAPT, MAJ, LTCOL

INITIAL TRAINING SETTING: FORMAL

CONDITION: Given a battalion task force or regimental combat team operating within a MAGTF/Joint/Combined/Interagency environment, higher headquarters' operations order, commander's guidance and references, in conjunction with the fire support coordinator, while implementing the orders process.

STANDARD: By developing a concept of fires and supporting orders products that accomplishes the mission and commander's intent.

PERFORMANCE STEPS:
1. Plan, coordinate and integrate the employment of supporting arms to support the scheme of maneuver.
2. Integrate direct and indirect fire weapons into fire plans.
3. Integrate the Fires/Effects capabilities of available joint, subordinate and supporting units.
4. Implement deliberate and reactive targeting processes to effectively attack crucial enemy functions and set the conditions for success.
5. Identify and assess threat fire support capabilities.
6. Synchronize fires/effects plan with IO plan.

REFERENCES:
1. ATP 4E w/CH 2 Allied Spotting Procedures for Naval Gunfire Support
2. MCRP 3-15.2A Tactical Employment of Mortars
3. MCRP 3-16.1A Tactics, Techniques and Procedures for Field Artillery Target Acquisition
4. MCRP 3-16.6 Multiservice Procedures for the Joint Application of Firepower (J-Fire)
5. MCWP 3-16 Fire Support Coordination in the Ground Combat Element
6. MCWP 3-16.1 Artillery Operations

7. MCWP 3-23.1 Close Air Support
8. MCWP 3-25.3 Marine Air Command and Control System Handbook
9. MCWP 3-40.4 MAGTF Information Operations

MISCELLANEOUS:

ADMINISTRATIVE INSTRUCTIONS: Performance steps are derived from tasks0302-FSPT-1301, 0302-FSPT-2301, 0302-FSPT-2302, 0302-OPS-2101, and Core Capability #18 from Weapons Company Commander, Infantry Battalion. See Infantry T&R Manual for additional information.

OTIC-PLAN-2005: Integrate information operations into ground combat operations

EVALUATION-CODED: NO   **SUSTAINMENT INTERVAL:** 6 months

MOS PERFORMING: 0203, 0302, 0303, 0306, 0313, 0321, 0369, 0802, 0848, 0861, 1302, 1371, 1802, 1803, 1812, 1833, 8007

BILLETS: Assistant Operations Officer, Fire Support Coordinator, Fires Chief, Gunner, Operations Chief, Operations Officer, Assistant Operations Chief

GRADES: GYSGT, MSGT, MGYSGT, CWO-2, CWO-3, CWO-4, CAPT, MAJ, LTCOL

INITIAL TRAINING SETTING: FORMAL

CONDITION: Given a battalion task force or regimental combat team operating within a MAGTF/Joint/Combined/Interagency environment, higher headquarters' operations order, commander's guidance and references, in conjunction with the information operations officer, while implementing the orders process.

STANDARD: By developing a concept of information operations and supporting orders products that accomplishes the mission and commander's intent.

PERFORMANCE STEPS:
1. Plan, coordinate and integrate the employment of information operations to support the scheme of maneuver.
2. Integrate the IO capabilities of available joint, subordinate and supporting units.
3. Implement deliberate and reactive targeting processes to effectively influence the operational environment and set the conditions for success.
4. Identify and assess threat IO capabilities.
5. Synchronize IO plan with fires/effects plan.
6. Recommend IO related information requirements as Commander's Critical Information Requirements.
7. Identify and coordinate external support required for IO.
8. Identify data required to assess IO effectiveness.
9. Synchronize IO plan with CMO plan.

REFERENCES:
1. JP 3-13 Joint Doctrine for Information Operations
2. MCWP 3-40.4 MAGTF Information Operations
3. NWP 3-13 Navy Information Operations

MISCELLANEOUS:

ADMINISTRATIVE INSTRUCTIONS: 1. Performance steps are derived from tasks: 9934-PLAN-1008, 9934-PLAN-1009, 9934-PLAN-1010, 9934-PLAN-1019, 9934-PLAN-1020, 9934-PLAN-1021, 9934-PLAN-1022, 9934-PLAN-1023, 9934-PLAN-1024, 9934-PLAN-1025, 9934-PLAN-1026, 9934-PLAN-1031, 9934-PLAN-1032, 9934-PLAN-1033,9934-PLAN-1034, 9934-PLAN-1035, 9934-PLAN-1036, 9934-PLAN-1037, 9934-PLAN-1038, 9934-PLAN-1039, 9934-PLAN-1040, 9934-PLAN-1041, 9934-PLAN-1042, 9934-PLAN-1043, 9934-PLAN-1047, and 9934-PLAN-1048. See Information Operations T&R Manual for additional information.

OTIC-PLAN-2006: Integrate civil military operations into ground combat operations

EVALUATION-CODED: NO   **SUSTAINMENT INTERVAL:** 6 months

MOS PERFORMING: 0203, 0302, 0303, 0306, 0313, 0321, 0369, 0802, 0848, 0861, 1302, 1371, 1802, 1803, 1812, 1833, 8007

BILLETS: Assistant Operations Officer, Fire Support Coordinator, Fires Chief, Gunner, Operations Chief, Operations Officer, Assistant Operations Chief

GRADES: GYSGT, MSGT, MGYSGT, CWO-2, CWO-3, CWO-4, CAPT, MAJ, LTCOL

INITIAL TRAINING SETTING: FORMAL

CONDITION: Given a battalion task force or regimental combat team operating within a MAGTF/Joint/Combined/Interagency environment, higher headquarters' operations order, commander's guidance and references, in conjunction with the civil affairs officer, while implementing the orders process.

STANDARD: Develop a concept of civil military operations and supporting orders products that accomplishes the mission and commander's intent.

PERFORMANCE STEPS:
1. Plan, coordinate and integrate the employment of civil military operations to support the concept of operations.
2. Integrate the CMO capabilities of available interagency organizations and joint, subordinate and supporting units.
3. Synchronize CMO plan with IO plan.
4. Identify desired CMO methods, media and products to support plans and orders.
5. Identify parameters and requirements to support CMO estimates/ assumptions.
6. Develop CMO related information requirements as Commander's Critical Information Requirements.

REFERENCES:
1. JP 3-57 Joint Doctrine for Civil Military Operations
2. NAVMC 3500.22 Civil Affairs T&R Manual
3. MCRP 3-33.1A Civil Affairs TTPs

MISCELLANEOUS:

ADMINISTRATIVE INSTRUCTIONS: 1. Performance steps are derived from tasks CAG-PLAN-3049 and CAG-PREP-3061. See Civil Affairs T&R Manual for additional information.

OTIC-PLAN-2007: Integrate logistics into ground combat operations

EVALUATION-CODED: NO   SUSTAINMENT INTERVAL: 6 months

MOS PERFORMING: 0203, 0302, 0303, 0306, 0313, 0321, 0369, 0802, 0848, 0861, 1302, 1371, 1802, 1803, 1812, 1833, 8007

BILLETS: Assistant Operations Officer, Fire Support Coordinator, Fires Chief, Gunner, Operations Chief, Operations Officer, Assistant Operations Chief

GRADES: GYSGT, MSGT, MGYSGT, CWO-2, CWO-3, CWO-4, CAPT, MAJ, LTCOL

INITIAL TRAINING SETTING: FORMAL

CONDITION: Given a battalion task force or regimental combat team operating within a MAGTF/Joint/Combined/Interagency environment, higher headquarters' operations order, commander's guidance and references, in coordination with the logistics officer, while implementing the orders process.

STANDARD: Develop a concept of logistics and supporting orders products that accomplishes the mission and commander's intent.

PERFORMANCE STEPS:
1. Plan, coordinate and integrate the employment of logistics to support the concept of operations.
2. Integrate the logistics capabilities of available coalition, host nation, interagency organizations and joint, subordinate and supporting units.
3. Identify desired methods, media, and products to support the logistics effort to the Marine Corps Planning Process.
4. Identify parameters and requirements for logistics estimates/assumptions.
5. Identify critical logistical information requirements that will significantly impact operations.
6. Identify and prioritize CSS requirements.

REFERENCES:
1. MCDP 4 Logistics
2. MCWP 4-1 Logistics Operations
3. MCWP 4-11 Tactical-Level Logistics
4. MCWP 4-11.4 Maintenance Operations
5. MCWP 4-11.7 MAGTF Supply Operations
6. MCWP 5-1 Marine Corps Planning Process

MISCELLANEOUS:

ADMINISTRATIVE INSTRUCTIONS: Performance steps are derived from task 0302-OPS-2102. See Infantry T&R Manual for additional information.

OTIC-PLAN-2008: Integrate communications into ground combat operations

EVALUATION-CODED: NO   SUSTAINMENT INTERVAL: 6 months

MOS PERFORMING: 0203, 0302, 0303, 0306, 0313, 0321, 0369, 0802, 0848, 0861, 1302, 1371, 1802, 1803, 1812, 1833, 8007

BILLETS: Assistant Operations Officer, Fire Support Coordinator, Fires Chief, Gunner, Operations Chief, Operations Officer, Assistant Operations Chief

GRADES: GYSGT, MSGT, MGYSGT, CWO-2, CWO-3, CWO-4, CAPT, MAJ, LTCOL

INITIAL TRAINING SETTING: FORMAL

CONDITION: Given a battalion task force or regimental combat team operating within a MAGTF/Joint/Combined/Interagency environment, higher headquarters' operations order, commander's guidance and references, in conjunction with the communications officer, while implementing the orders process.

STANDARD: Develop a concept of communications and supporting orders products that accomplishes the mission and commander's intent.

PERFORMANCE STEPS:
1. Plan, coordinate and integrate the employment of communications to support the concept of operations.
2. Identify desired methods, media, and products to support communications planning and orders.
3. Determine and prioritize commander's communication requirements.
4. Identify and integrate the capabilities of organic and relevant, non-organic communication assets in support of the concept of operation.
5. Identify the tenants of communications
6. Identify communication readiness resource concerns.
7. Identify elements of communications security.
8. Identify elements of information assurance.

REFERENCES:
1. MCDP 1-0 Marine Corps Operations
2. MCDP 6 Command and Control
3. MCWP 3-40.1 Marine Air-Ground Task Force Command and Control
4. MCWP 3-40.3 Communications and Information Systems
5. MCWP 5-1 Marine Corps Planning Process

MISCELLANEOUS:

ADMINISTRATIVE INSTRUCTIONS: Performance steps are derived from tasks 0602-PLAN-1101, 0602-MNGT-1701, 0602-MNGT-1702, and 0603-PLAN-2101. See Communication T&R Manual for additional information.

OTIC-PLAN-2009: Integrate force protection into ground combat operations

EVALUATION-CODED: NO   **SUSTAINMENT INTERVAL:** 6 months

MOS PERFORMING: 0203, 0302, 0303, 0306, 0313, 0321, 0369, 0802, 0848, 0861, 1302, 1371, 1802, 1803, 1812, 1833, 8007

BILLETS: Assistant Operations Officer, Fire Support Coordinator, Fires Chief, Gunner, Operations Chief, Operations Officer, Assistant Operations Chief

GRADES: GYSGT, MSGT, MGYSGT, CWO-2, CWO-3, CWO-4, CAPT, MAJ, LTCOL

INITIAL TRAINING SETTING: FORMAL

CONDITION: Given a battalion task force or regimental combat team operating within a MAGTF/Joint/Combined/Interagency environment, higher headquarters' operations order, commander's guidance and references, in conjunction with the force protection and intelligence officers, while implementing the orders process.

STANDARD: Identify the threat and resource requirements, and develop the plan to mitigate risk to friendly forces.

PERFORMANCE STEPS:
1. Integrate Force Protection assessments and planning considerations into the planning process.
2. Identify requirements for security plan development.
3. Identify requirements for antiterrorism plan development.
4. Identify requirements for contingency response options and consequence management procedures.
5. Identify requirements for logistical support of force protection plan implementation.
6. Supervise coordination with host nation/local authorities as required.

REFERENCES:
1. JP 3-07.2 JTTP for Antiterrorism
2. MCDP 1-0 Marine Corps Operations
3. MCWP 3-40.1 Marine Air-Ground Task Force Command and Control
4. MCWP 3-40.3 Communications and Information Systems
5. MCWP 5-1 Marine Corps Planning Process
6. NAVMC 2927 Antiterrorism/Force Protection Campaign Plan
7. MCWP 2-6 Counterintelligence

MISCELLANEOUS:

ADMINISTRATIVE INSTRUCTIONS: Performance steps are derived from tasks: ATO-PLAN-1040, ATO-PLAN-1041, ATO-PLAN-1042, ATO-PLAN-1043, ATO-PLAN-1044, ATO-PLAN-1045, ATO-PLAN-1046, and ATO-PLAN-1047. See Antiterrorism Officer T&R Manual for additional information.

OTIC-PLAN-2010: Integrate MAGTF support into ground combat operations

EVALUATION-CODED: NO   **SUSTAINMENT INTERVAL**: 6 months

MOS PERFORMING: 0203, 0302, 0303, 0306, 0313, 0321, 0369, 0802, 0848, 0861, 1302, 1371, 1802, 1803, 1812, 1833, 8007

BILLETS: Assistant Operations Officer, Fire Support Coordinator, Fires Chief, Gunner, Operations Chief, Operations Officer, Assistant Operations Chief

GRADES: GYSGT, MSGT, MGYSGT, CWO-2, CWO-3, CWO-4, CAPT, MAJ, LTCOL

INITIAL TRAINING SETTING: FORMAL

CONDITION: Given a battalion task force or regimental combat team operating within a MAGTF/Joint/Combined/Interagency environment, higher headquarters' operations order, commander's guidance and references, while implementing the orders process.

STANDARD: GCE concept of operations supported by MAGTF units, assets, and capabilities in accordance with the mission and commander's intent

PERFORMANCE STEPS:
1. Identify the organization, capabilities, employment procedures, and support requirements of all elements of the MAGTF.
2. Identify requirements for MAGTF support to ground combat operations.
3. Integrate Aviation Combat Element capabilities into ground combat operations.
4. Implement procedures for the integration of the Logistics Combat Element into ground combat operations.
5. Implement procedures for the integration of MAGTF intelligence, surveillance, and reconnaissance into ground combat operations.
6. Implement procedures for the integration of MAGTF command and control capabilities into ground combat operations.
7. Receive and integrate MAGTF attachments into the GCE.
8. Establish liaisons with MAGTF elements.

REFERENCES:
1. MCWP 3-1 Ground Combat Operations
2. MCWP 3-40.1 Marine Air-Ground Task Force Command and Control
3. MCWP 3-40.8 Componency
4. MCWP 3-43.3 MAGTF Fires (Draft dtd 20 Dec 2002)
5. FMI 5-0.1 The Operations Process
6. MCWP 3-33.5 Counter Insurgency Operations
7. Tentative Manual for Countering Irregular Threats

MISCELLANEOUS:

ADMINISTRATIVE INSTRUCTIONS: The following references provide additional amplifying documentation: 1. Military Support to Stabilization, Security, Transition, and Reconstruction Operations Joint Operating Concept, US Joint Forces Command 20062. Insights on Joint Operations: The Art and Science Best Practices. The Move toward Coherently Integrated Joint, Interagency, and Multinational Operations by GEN (Ret) Gary Luck, Senior Mentor, Joint Warfighting Center, U.S. Joint Forces Command.

OTIC-PLAN-2011: Integrate joint, interagency, and coalition support into GCE operations.

EVALUATION-CODED: NO   **SUSTAINMENT INTERVAL**: 6 months

MOS PERFORMING: 0203, 0302, 0303, 0306, 0313, 0321, 0369, 0802, 0848, 0861, 1302, 1371, 1802, 1803, 1812, 1833, 8007

BILLETS: Assistant Operations Officer, Fire Support Coordinator, Fires Chief, Gunner, Operations Chief, Operations Officer, Assistant Operations Chief

GRADES: GYSGT, MSGT, MGYSGT, CWO-2, CWO-3, CWO-4, CAPT, MAJ, LTCOL

INITIAL TRAINING SETTING: FORMAL

CONDITION: Given a battalion task force or regimental combat team operating within a MAGTF/Joint/Combined/Interagency environment, higher headquarters' operations order, commander's guidance and references, while implementing the orders process.

STANDARD: GCE concept of operations supported by joint, interagency, and coalition organizations, assets, and capabilities in accordance with the mission and commander's intent.

PERFORMANCE STEPS:
1. Identify the organization, capabilities, employment procedures, and support requirements of key joint, interagency, and coalition organizations and capacities.
2. Identify requirements for joint, interagency, and coalition support for the concept of operation.
3. Integrate joint, interagency, and coalition organizations and assets into the concept of operation.
4. Receive and integrate joint, interagency, and coalition attachments into the GCE battlespace.
5. Establish liaisons with joint, interagency and coalition organizations.

REFERENCES:
1. NSPD 44 Management of Interagency Efforts Concerning Reconstruction and Stabilization
2. DoDD 3000.5, Military Support for Stability, Security, Transition, and Reconstruction (SSTR) Operations
3. JP 3-0 Joint Operations
4. MCWP 3-1 Ground Combat Operations
5. MCWP 3-40.8 Componency
6. MCWP 3-43.3 MAGTF Fires (Draft dtd 20 Dec 2002)
7. FMI 5-0.1 The Operations Process
8. MCWP 3-33.5 Counter Insurgency Operations
9. Tentative Manual for Countering Irregular Threats

MISCELLANEOUS:

ADMINISTRATIVE INSTRUCTIONS: The following references provide additional amplifying documentation:
1. Military Support to Stabilization, Security, Transition, and Reconstruction Operations Joint Operating Concept, US Joint Forces Command 2006.
2. Insights on Joint Operations: The Art and Science Best Practices.
3. The Move toward Coherently Integrated Joint, Interagency, and Multinational Operations by GEN (Ret) Gary Luck, Senior Mentor, Joint Warfighting Center, U.S. Joint Forces Command.

OTIC-PLAN-2012: Develop an Information Management (IM) Plan

EVALUATION-CODED: NO   **SUSTAINMENT INTERVAL:** 12 months

MOS PERFORMING: 0202, 0203, 0231, 0302, 0303, 0306, 0313, 0321, 0369, 0402, 0491, 0802, 0848, 0861, 1302, 1371, 1802, 1803, 1812, 1833

BILLETS: Assistant Operations Officer, Fire Support Coordinator, Gunner, Operations Chief, Operations Officer, Assistant Operations Chief

GRADES: GYSGT, MSGT, MGYSGT, CWO-2, CWO-3, CWO-4, CAPT, MAJ, LTCOL

INITIAL TRAINING SETTING: FORMAL

CONDITION: Given all the elements of a Combat Operation Center, a Battalion Task Force or Regimental Combat Team operating within a MAGTF/Joint/Combined/ Interagency environment, a higher headquarters' operations order, Commander's guidance and references.

STANDARD: To facilitate information flow and enhance rapid and timely decision making.

PERFORMANCE STEPS:
1. Determine Information Exchange Requirements (IER's) for the staff and commander of each echelon
2. Determine how to support the staff and commander to meet IER's for each echelon using C4ISR systems within the framework of the battle process.
3. Manage CCIR's.
4. Develop the information management plan for each echelon

REFERENCES:
1. FM 3-0 Operations
2. FMI 5-0.1 The Operations Process
3. MCDP 1-0 Marine Corps Operations
4. MCWP 3-1 Ground Combat Operations
5. MCWP 3-40.2 MAGTF Information Management

MISCELLANEOUS:

ADMINISTRATIVE INSTRUCTIONS: This task will be conducted in accordance with OTIC 01.01-09 performance steps.

SUPPORT REQUIREMENTS: MCTOG Battle Lab

OTIC-PLAN-2101: Participate in the Marine Corps Planning Process.

EVALUATION-CODED: NO   **SUSTAINMENT INTERVAL:** 6 months

MOS PERFORMING: 0313, 0321, 0369, 0848, 0861, 1371, 1812, 1833

BILLETS: Fires Chief, Operations Chief, Assistant Operations Chief

GRADES: GYSGT, MSGT, MGYSGT

INITIAL TRAINING SETTING: FORMAL

CONDITION: Given a battalion task force or regimental combat team operating within a MAGTF/Joint/Combined/Interagency environment, higher headquarters' order, commander's guidance and references, while implementing the orders process.

STANDARD: Produce plans and orders products which support the accomplishment of the mission and commander's intent.

PERFORMANCE STEPS:
1. Assist in mission analysis.
2. Assist in the development of courses of action.
3. Assist in wargaming of courses of action.
4. Assist in comparison and recommendation of courses of action.
5. Assist in development of appropriate staff products, operations plans, orders, annexes, and appendices.
6. Assist in transition by compiling the components of an operations order for distribution to subordinate units.

REFERENCES:
1. MCWP 3-40.1 Marine Air-Ground Task Force Command and Control
2. MCWP 5-1 Marine Corps Planning Process

MISCELLANEOUS:

ADMINISTRATIVE INSTRUCTIONS: Performance steps are derived from task 0502-PLAN-1016. See MAGTF Plans Officer T&R Manual for additional information.

OTIC-TRNG-2001: Manage unit training

EVALUATION-CODED: NO   **SUSTAINMENT INTERVAL:** 3 months

MOS PERFORMING: 0203, 0302, 0303, 0306, 0313, 0321, 0369, 0802, 0848, 0861, 1302, 1371, 1802, 1803, 1812, 1833

BILLETS: Assistant Operations Officer, Fire Support Coordinator, Fires Chief, Marine Gunner, Operations Chief, Operations Officer, Assistant Operations Chief

GRADES: GYSGT, MSGT, MGYSGT, CWO-2, CWO-3, CWO-4, CAPT, MAJ, LTCOL

INITIAL TRAINING SETTING: FORMAL

CONDITION: Given a unit, commander's guidance, METL, T&R Manuals, required external support and equipment, and references.

STANDARD: Conducting standards based training, developing the required plans, calendars, and schedules to validate unit training plans to support MET proficiency.

PERFORMANCE STEPS:
1. Analyze Higher Headquarters' Mission Essential Task List (METL) in order to determine subordinate units' tasks.
2. Derive tasks from higher headquarters' Mission Essential Task List and translate into subordinate units' METs.
3. Identify core METs from associated T&R Manuals.
4. Develop training that supports subordinate units' METs.
5. Determine and procure requirements that support the training plan.
6. Execute training, evaluation, and remediation.

REFERENCES:
1. MCO 1553.1A The Systems Approach to Training
2. MCRP 3-0A Unit Training Management Guide
3. MCRP 3-0B How To Conduct Training

MISCELLANEOUS:

ADMINISTRATIVE INSTRUCTIONS:
1. Task is derived from task 0302-TRNG-2101. See Infantry T&R Manual for additional information.
2. This applies to all combat arms METs and references.

OTIC-TRNG-2002: Conduct training

EVALUATION-CODED: NO   **SUSTAINMENT INTERVAL:** 3 months

MOS PERFORMING: 0203, 0302, 0303, 0306, 0313, 0321, 0369, 0802, 0848, 0861, 1302, 1371, 1802, 1803, 1812, 1833

BILLETS: Assistant Operations Officer, Fire Support Coordinator, Fires Chief, Marine Gunner, Operations Chief, Operations Officer, Assistant Operations Chief

GRADES: GYSGT, MSGT, MGYSGT, CWO-2, CWO-3, CWO-4, CAPT, MAJ, LTCOL

INITIAL TRAINING SETTING: FORMAL

CONDITION: Given a unit, commander's guidance, a METL, T&R Manuals, required external support and equipment, and references.

STANDARD: Ensure each Marine and/or unit achieves the training standard, and prepares the unit for future combat operations in accordance with the references.

PERFORMANCE STEPS:
1. Use developed METs to determine the training tasks.
2. Identify and request the required resources.
3. Prepare a training concept.
4. Define the training objectives.
5. Integrate logistical support and C2 into training plan.
6. Incorporate ORM into the training plan.
7. Conduct the instruction.
8. Evaluate training IAW appropriate T&R manual.
9. Plan for remediation as required.
10. Update individual training records.

REFERENCES:
1. MCO 1553.1A The Systems Approach to Training
2. MCRP 3-0A Unit Training Management Guide
3. MCRP 3-0B How To Conduct Training

MISCELLANEOUS:

ADMINISTRATIVE INSTRUCTIONS: Task is derived from task 0302-TRNG-2201.

OTIC-TRNG-2003: Prepare a unit for combat

EVALUATION-CODED: NO   **SUSTAINMENT INTERVAL:** 3 months

MOS PERFORMING: 0203, 0302, 0303, 0306, 0313, 0321, 0369, 0802, 0848, 0861, 1302, 1371, 1802, 1803, 1812, 1833

BILLETS: Assistant Operations Officer, Fire Support Coordinator, Fires Chief, Marine Gunner, Operations Chief, Operations Officer, Assistant Operations Chief

GRADES: GYSGT, MSGT, MGYSGT, CWO-2, CWO-3, CWO-4, CAPT, MAJ, LTCOL

INITIAL TRAINING SETTING: FORMAL

CONDITION: Given a unit, commander's guidance, required external support and equipment, a requirement to achieve combat readiness, METL and T&R Manuals, and references.

STANDARD: Ensure SOPs are developed, training plans are in place to achieve MET proficiency, and DRRS reports have been submitted in accordance with the references.

PERFORMANCE STEPS:
1. Prepare combat standard operating procedures.

2. Prepare and prioritize mission specific requirements.
3. Provide inputs and oversight of the DRRS report.
4. Create a battalion/regimental pre-deployment training plan.
5. Develop and implement validation of combat standard operation procedures.
6. Supervise the remediation plans.

REFERENCES:
1. MCO 1553.1A The Systems Approach to Training
2. MCRP 3-0A Unit Training Management Guide
3. MCRP 3-0B How To Conduct Training

MISCELLANEOUS:

ADMINISTRATIVE INSTRUCTIONS: Performance steps are derived from tasks is derived from tasks 0302-TRNG-2101 and 0302-TRNG-2201. See Infantry T&R Manual for additional information.

OTIC-TRNG-2004: Establish Information Management Training Requirements

EVALUATION-CODED: NO

SUSTAINMENT INTERVAL: 6 months

MOS PERFORMING: 0202, 0203, 0231, 0302, 0303, 0306, 0313, 0321, 0369, 0402, 0491, 0802, 0848, 0861, 1302, 1371, 1802, 1803, 1812, 1833

BILLETS: Intelligence Officer, Assistant Operations Officer, Fire Support Coordinator, Marine Gunner, Operations Chief, Operations Officer, Logistics Officer, Air Officer, Watch Officer, Assistant Operations Chief

GRADES: GYSGT, MSGT, MGYSGT, CWO-2, CWO-3, CWO-4, CAPT, MAJ, LTCOL

INITIAL TRAINING SETTING: FORMAL

CONDITION: Given all the elements of a Combat Operation Center, a Battalion Task Force or Regimental Combat Team training to be prepared to operate in a MAGTF/Joint/Combined/ Interagency environment, Commander's guidance and references.

STANDARD: Develop a training plan that provides a staff the ability to distill information, provide relevant and timely assessments and create an operational picture that provides a Commander with situational awareness; accelerating his ability to make decisions.

PERFORMANCE STEPS:
1. Analyze the IM training requirements for relevant doctrinal staff battle processes and the training requirements for the C4ISR applications that support the staff in the execution of doctrinal battle process.
2. Identify IM standards from the references and write standards if none already exist.
3. Design an IM training plan for the staff.
4. Leverage training resources.
5. Train staff in doctrinal staff battle process and the use of C4ISR

systems in support of those processes using battle drills.

6. Assess the effectiveness of staff in the execution of battle drills.
7. Conduct evaluation, after action review, and debrief.
8. Create training programs for new staff battle processes and C4ISR systems based on established training standards and mission analysis.

REFERENCES:
1. FM 3-0 Operations
2. FMI 5-0.1 The Operations Process
3. MCDP 1-0 Marine Corps Operations
4. MCWP 3-1 Ground Combat Operations
5. MCWP 3-40.2 MAGTF Information Management

OTIC-TRNG-2201: Design a training program

EVALUATION-CODED: NO   **SUSTAINMENT INTERVAL:** 3 months

MOS PERFORMING: 0306

BILLETS: Marine Gunner

GRADES: CWO-2, CWO-3, CWO-4

INITIAL TRAINING SETTING: FORMAL

CONDITION: Given a unit, commander's guidance, a METL, T&R Manuals, required external support and equipment, and references.

STANDARD: To design training programs, schedule training, and execute training at the battalion/regiment level, evaluating the performance of tasks that support METs in accordance with the references.

PERFORMANCE STEPS:
1. Assist in the mission analysis for the training program.
2. Analyze training requirements, including combat skills training for non-infantry MOSs.
3. Identify standards from the references.
4. Design a training plan for a specified unit.
5. Identify, manage, and coordinate training resources.
6. Monitor qualification of individual and crew served weapons.
7. Conduct after-action reviews and debriefs.
8. Monitor evaluation process of the training program.
9. Create training programs for new weapons/equipment based on established training standards and mission analysis.

REFERENCES:
1. MCO 1553.1A The Systems Approach to Training
2. MCRP 3-0A Unit Training Management Guide
3. MCRP 3-0B How To Conduct Training

MISCELLANEOUS:

ADMINISTRATIVE INSTRUCTIONS: Performance steps are derived from tasks 0302-TRNG-2101 and 0302-TRNG-2201. See Infantry T&R Manual for additional information.

OTIC-TRNG-2202: Integrate GCE weapons capabilities into training programs

EVALUATION-CODED: NO   SUSTAINMENT INTERVAL: 6 months

MOS PERFORMING: 0306

BILLETS: Marine Gunner

GRADES: CWO-2, CWO-3, CWO-4

INITIAL TRAINING SETTING: FORMAL

CONDITION: Given a unit, commander's guidance, a METL, T&R Manuals, required external support and equipment, and references.

STANDARD: Establish and execute weapons training programs in preparation for deployment and GCE operations in accordance with the references.

PERFORMANCE STEPS:
1. Identify and assess GCE weapons employment capabilities and limitations.
2. Integrate GCE weapons safety considerations into the planning process.
3. Identify and integrate GCE pre-deployment weapons training requirements.

REFERENCES:
1. MCO 1553.1A The Systems Approach to Training
2. MCRP 3-0A Unit Training Management Guide
3. MCRP 3-0B How To Conduct Training

MISCELLANEOUS:

ADMINISTRATIVE INSTRUCTIONS: The OTI Marine Gunner maintains currency in the emerging concepts, doctrine, and training requirements.

OTIC-TRNG-2203: Integrate threat weapons capabilities into training programs

EVALUATION-CODED: NO   SUSTAINMENT INTERVAL: 6 months

MOS PERFORMING: 0306

BILLETS: Marine Gunner

GRADES: CWO-2, CWO-3, CWO-4

INITIAL TRAINING SETTING: FORMAL

CONDITION: Given a unit, commander's guidance, a METL, T&R Manuals, required external support and equipment, and references.

STANDARD: Establish and execute threat weapons training programs in preparation for deployment and GCE operations in accordance with the references.

PERFORMANCE STEPS:
1. Identify and assess threat weapons employment capabilities and limitations.
2. Integrate threat weapons considerations into the planning process.
3. Identify and integrate threat weapons pre-deployment training requirements.

REFERENCES:
1. MCO 1553.1A The Systems Approach to Training
2. MCRP 3-0A Unit Training Management Guide
3. MCRP 3-0B How To Conduct Training

MISCELLANEOUS:

ADMINISTRATIVE INSTRUCTIONS: The OTI Marine Gunner maintains currency in the emerging concepts, doctrine, and training requirements.

OTIC-OPS-2001: Establish a Command Post

EVALUATION-CODED: NO   **SUSTAINMENT INTERVAL**: 6 months

MOS PERFORMING: 0203, 0302, 0303, 0306, 0313, 0321, 0369, 0802, 0848, 0861, 1302, 1371, 1802, 1803, 1812, 1833

BILLETS: Assistant Operations Officer, Fire Support Coordinator, Marine Gunner, Operations Chief, Operations Officer, Assistant Operations Chief

GRADES: GYSGT, MSGT, MGYSGT, CWO-2, CWO-3, CWO-4, CAPT, MAJ, LTCOL

INITIAL TRAINING SETTING: FORMAL

CONDITION: Given all the elements of a command post, a battalion task force or regimental combat team operating within a MAGTF/Joint/Combined/Interagency environment, a higher headquarters' operations order and commander's guidance

STANDARD: Integrate systems, personnel and processes to efficiently command and control ground combat operations.

PERFORMANCE STEPS:
1. Organize the staff and configure command post echelons to support mission accomplishment.
2. Establish and implement procedures for reconnaissance, selection, and occupation of positions.
3. Establish and implement procedures to conduct movement.
4. Direct the security and organization of the command post area.
5. Establish communications with higher, adjacent and supporting units
6. Establish a battle rhythm.
7. Transition control of operations to the appropriate echelon.

REFERENCES:
1. FM 3-0 Operations
2. FMI 5-0.1 The Operations Process
3. MCDP 1-0 Marine Corps Operations
4. MCWP 3-1 Ground Combat Operations

MISCELLANEOUS:

ADMINISTRATIVE INSTRUCTIONS: Detailed operator skills for supporting systems are not necessary, but an understanding of operator skills is required to complete this task to standard.

OTIC-OPS-2002: Implement orders process

EVALUATION-CODED: NO   SUSTAINMENT INTERVAL: 6 months

MOS PERFORMING: 0203, 0302, 0303, 0306, 0802, 1302, 1802, 1803

BILLETS: Assistant Operations Officer, Fire Support Coordinator, Marine Gunner, Operations Officer

GRADES: CWO-2, CWO-3, CWO-4, CAPT, MAJ, LTCOL

INITIAL TRAINING SETTING: FORMAL

CONDITION: Given a battalion task force or regimental combat team operating within a MAGTF/Joint/Combined/Interagency environment.

STANDARD: GCE mission executed in accordance with the commander's intent.

PERFORMANCE STEPS:
1. Receive HHQ order, CBAE, and commander's guidance
2. Determine planning timeline, associated planning methodology, and required orders products
3. Issue warning orders
4. Conduct staff planning and synchronization
5. Coordinate operations and required support with higher, adjacent, subordinate and supporting units
6. Issue required orders
7. Conduct confirmation briefs
8. Coordinate and conduct required rehearsals
9. Supervise unit preparation for mission execution
10. Direct combat operations

REFERENCES:
1. MCWP 3-1 Ground Combat Operations
2. MCWP 3-40.1 Marine Air-Ground Task Force Command and Control
3. FMI 5-0.1 The Operations Process
4. MCWP 5-1 Marine Corps Planning Process
5. MCRP 3-11.1a Commander's Tactical Handbook
6. MCRP 5-12a Operational Terms & Graphics

MISCELLANEOUS:

ADMINISTRATIVE INSTRUCTIONS: Additional amplifying documentation may be found in the references.

OTIC-OPS-2003: Exercise command and control during ground combat operations

EVALUATION-CODED: NO   **SUSTAINMENT INTERVAL:** 6 months

MOS PERFORMING: 0302, 0303, 0313, 0321, 0369, 0802, 0848, 0861, 1302, 1371, 1802, 1803, 1812, 1833

BILLETS: Assistant Operations Officer, Fire Support Coordinator, Operations Officer, Fires Chief, Operations Chief, Assistant Operations Chief

GRADES: GYSGT, MSGT, MGYSGT, CAPT, MAJ, LTCOL

INITIAL TRAINING SETTING: FORMAL

CONDITION: Given a battalion task force or regimental combat team operating within a MAGTF/Joint/Combined/Interagency environment, higher headquarters' operations order, commander's guidance and references, while implementing the orders process.

STANDARD: Through battle management and the functional area requirements of staff operations the commander is able to make informed decisions to conduct effective unit operations.

PERFORMANCE STEPS:
1. Organize and configure the command post.
2. Synchronize intelligence, fires, maneuver, and logistics to achieve combined arms effects against the threat.
3. Maintain communications with higher, adjacent, supporting units and organizations.
4. Conduct battle management.
5. Implement the information management plan.
6. Conduct operational assessment and combat reporting.
7. Establish, evaluate and manage force protection posture as situation dictates (MOPP, Air Defense, ROE, and Readiness Conditions/Alert Status).
8. Conduct contingency response, QRF response, or commit the reserve.
9. Develop and issue fragmentary orders and future plans as situation dictates.

REFERENCES:
1. FM 3-0 Operations
2. FM 3-90 Tactics
3. FMI 5-0.1 The Operations Process
4. MCDP 1-0 Marine Corps Operations
5. MCWP 3-1 Ground Combat Operations
6. MCWP 3-16 Fire Support Coordination in the Ground Combat Element
7. MCWP 5-1 Marine Corps Planning Process

SUPPORT REQUIREMENTS: Combat Operations Center Battle Lab

OTIC-OPS-2004: Integrate and synchronize the intelligence effort to support combat operations.

EVALUATION-CODED: NO   **SUSTAINMENT INTERVAL:** 6 months

MOS PERFORMING: 0202, 0203, 0302, 0303, 0306, 0802, 1302, 1802, 1803

BILLETS: Assistant Operations Officer, Fire Support Coordinator, Marine Gunner, Operations Officer

GRADES: CWO-2, CWO-3, CWO-4, CAPT, MAJ, LTCOL

INITIAL TRAINING SETTING: FORMAL

CONDITION: Given a battalion task force or regimental combat team operating within a MAGTF/Joint/Combined/Interagency environment, higher headquarters' operations order, commander's guidance and references, while implementing the orders process.

STANDARD: The commander is able to make informed decisions to conduct effective unit operations.

PERFORMANCE STEPS:
1. Direct the continued assessment of the threat center of gravity analysis
2. Focus the continued development of the IPOE
3. Direct the targeting effort by identifying critical threat functions to be attacked
4. Participate in the continued assessment of threat capabilities and intentions and the associated indicators and warnings.
5. Focus the continued assessment and prioritization of PIRs / IRs
6. Participate in the planning and coordination of tactical intelligence collection
7. Participate in combat assessment
8. Facilitate tactical debriefing, forensics, reporting, intelligence exploitation and site exploitation.

REFERENCES:
1. JP 2-01 Joint and National Intelligence Support to Military Operations
2. MCDP 1-0 Marine Corps Operations
3. MCRP 2-3A Intelligence Preparation of the Battlefield
4. MCWP 2-3 MAGTF Intelligence Production and Analysis
5. MCWP 2-6 Counterintelligence
6. MCWP 5-1 Marine Corps Planning Process
7. MSTP Pamphlet 2-0.1 The Red Cell

MISCELLANEOUS:

ADMINISTRATIVE INSTRUCTIONS: Additional amplifying documentation may be found in the references.

OTIC-OPS-2005: Execute the Information Management (IM) Plan

EVALUATION-CODED: NO   **SUSTAINMENT INTERVAL:** 6 months

MOS PERFORMING: 0203, 0231, 0302, 0303, 0306, 0313, 0321, 0369, 0402, 0491, 0802, 0848, 0861, 1302, 1371, 1802, 1803, 1812, 1833

BILLETS: Intelligence Officer, Assistant Operations Officer, Fire Support Coordinator, Marine Gunner, Operations Chief, Operations Officer, Logistics Officer, Air Officer, Watch Officer, Assistant Operations Chief

GRADES: GYSGT, MSGT, MGYSGT, CWO-2, CWO-3, CWO-4, CAPT, MAJ, LTCOL

INITIAL TRAINING SETTING: FORMAL

CONDITION: Given all the elements of a Combat Operation Center, a Battalion Task Force or Regimental Combat Team operating within a MAGTF/Joint/Combined/ Interagency environment, a higher headquarters' operations order, Commander's guidance and references.

STANDARD: Based on doctrinal staff battle processes and fielded C4ISR programs, execute an IM Plan in accordance with the references.

PERFORMANCE STEPS:
1. Execute the IM Plan for each echelon based on the Staff and Commanders' Information Exchange Requirements (IER's) and support requirements.
2. In a dynamic environment, assess the effectiveness of the IM plan in support of the staff and Commander's IER's and the ability of the staff to create situational awareness for the Commander.
3. Based on the student's assessment of his IM plan, modify the plan to best support the staff and commander with the goal of accelerating the commander's ability to make decisions faster than his enemy.

REFERENCES:
1. FM 3-0 Operations
2. FMI 5-0.1 The Operations Process
3. MCDP 1-0 Marine Corps Operations
4. MCWP 3-1 Ground Combat Operations
5. MCWP 3-40.2 MAGTF Information Management

SUPPORT REQUIREMENTS: MCTOG Battle Lab

OTIC-OPS-2006: Execute duties of Fire Support Coordinator

EVALUATION-CODED: NO   **SUSTAINMENT INTERVAL:** 6 months

MOS PERFORMING: 0203, 0302, 0303, 0306, 0802, 1302, 1802, 1803

BILLETS: Operations Officer, Assistant Operations Officer, Fire Support Coordinator, Marine Gunner

GRADES: CWO-2, CWO-3, CWO-4, CAPT, MAJ, LTCOL

INITIAL TRAINING SETTING: FORMAL

CONDITION: Given all the elements of a Fire Support Coordination Center, a battalion task force or regimental combat team operating within a

MAGTF/Joint/Combined/Interagency environment, a higher headquarters' operations order, commander's guidance and references.

STANDARD: Facilitate the integration of fires to support the scheme of maneuver.

PERFORMANCE STEPS:
1. Operate a Fire Support Coordination Center.
2. Provide technical and tactical oversight of the Fire Support Team coordinating the efforts of the Artillery and Naval Gunfire Liaison Teams, and Tactical Air Control Party in support of the commander's intent for fire support.
3. Develop required fire support documents to support the concept of operation.
4. Integrate supporting fires in accomplishment of commander's intent.
5. Deconflict and clear fires to ensure they are in support of maneuver.
6. Conduct deliberate and reactive targeting to effectively attack crucial enemy functions in accordance with the commander's priorities.
7. Synchronize non-kinetic effects with maneuver and fires.

REFERENCES:
1. ATP 4E w/CH 2 Allied Spotting Procedures for Naval Gunfire Support
2. FMFM 2-7 Fire Support in MAGTF Operations
3. MCRP 3-15.2A Tactical Employment of Mortars
4. MCRP 3-16.1A Tactics, Techniques and Procedures for Field Artillery Target Acquisition
5. MCRP 3-16.6 Multiservice Procedures for the Joint Application of Firepower (J-Fires)
6. MCWP 3-16 Fire Support Coordination in the Ground Combat Element
7. MCWP 3-16.1 Artillery Operations
8. MCWP 3-23.1 Close Air Support
9. MCWP 3-25.3 Marine Air Command and Control System Handbook
10. MCWP 3-40.4 MAGTF Information Operations

SUPPORT REQUIREMENTS:
1. Combined Arms Staff Trainer (CAST)
2. Combat Operations Center Battle Lab

MISCELLANEOUS:

ADMINISTRATIVE INSTRUCTIONS:
1. Live fire is not necessary if adequate computer simulation can be generated.
2. Performance steps are derived from tasks 0302-FSPT-1302, 0302-FSPT-1303, 0302-FSPT-2201, and Core Capability #15 from Weapons Company Commander, Infantry Battalion. Task is derived from Core Capability #19 from Weapons Company Commander, Infantry Battalion. See Infantry T&R Manual for additional information.

OTIC-OPS-2101: Execute duties of an Operations Chief

EVALUATION-CODED: NO   **SUSTAINMENT INTERVAL:** 6 months

MOS PERFORMING: 0313, 0321, 0369, 0848, 0861, 1371, 1812, 1833

BILLETS: Operations Chief, Assistant Operations Chief

GRADES: GYSGT, MSGT, MGYSGT

INITIAL TRAINING SETTING: FORMAL

CONDITION: Given all the elements of a command post, a battalion task force or regimental combat team operating within a MAGTF/Joint/Combined/Interagency environment, a higher headquarters' operations order, commander's guidance and references.

STANDARD: Facilitate the integration of systems, personnel and processes to effectively command and control an operation.

PERFORMANCE STEPS:
1. Supervise the emplacement and displacement of the command post.
2. Supervise layout, integration of systems and information exchange requirements throughout the command post to support integrated staff operations.
3. Manage and supervise the operations of a command post.
4. Organize C4ISR assets in the combat operations center.
5. Manage information flow through the combat operations center.
6. Supervise the input of data into the command journal.
7. Ensure the common operational picture (COP) is maintained.
8. Assist in the training of watch section personnel.
9. Supervise the accuracy and timely submission of messages and reports.
10. Assist in the preparation of products in support of the operations section.

REFERENCES:
1. FM 3-0 Operations
2. FMI 5-0.1 The Operations Process
3. MCDP 1-0 Marine Corps Operations
4. MCWP 3-1 Ground Combat Operations

SUPPORT REQUIREMENTS: Combat Operations Center Battle Lab

MISCELLANEOUS:

ADMINISTRATIVE INSTRUCTIONS: 1. Detailed operator skills for supporting systems are not necessary, but an understanding of operator skills is required to complete this task to standard. 2. Performance steps are derived from task 0369-OPS-2601 and 0369 Operations Chief, S-3 Section, Infantry Battalion/Regiment billet description. See Infantry T&R Manual for additional information.

OTIC-OPS-2102: Execute duties of Fires Chief

EVALUATION-CODED: NO   **SUSTAINMENT INTERVAL:** 6 months

MOS PERFORMING: 0313, 0321, 0369, 0848, 0861, 1371

BILLETS: Fires Chief

GRADES: GYSGT, MSGT, MGYSGT

INITIAL TRAINING SETTING: FORMAL

CONDITION: Given all the elements of a Fire Support Coordination Center, a battalion task force or regimental combat team operating within a MAGTF/Joint/Combined/Interagency environment, a higher headquarters' operations order, commander's guidance and references.

STANDARD: Facilitate the integration of fires to support the scheme of maneuver.

PERFORMANCE STEPS:
1. Supervise the emplacement and displacement of the Fire Support Coordination Center.
2. Manage the operations of a fire support coordination center.
3. Organize C4ISR assets in the fire support coordination center.
4. Supervise and coordinate the development of supporting arms plans.
5. Assist supporting arms representatives in the development of Fire Support Coordination Measures.
6. Maintain displays and overlays that support situational awareness to rapidly clear fires.
7. Supervise the input of data into the fire mission log.
8. Provide technical and tactical oversight to Fire Support Teams.
9. Assist in the integration of supporting arms fires.
10. Assist in the integration of direct and indirect fire weapons into fire plans.
11. Assist and coordinate the synchronization of non-kinetic fires with maneuver and fires.

REFERENCES:
1. ATP 4E w/CH 2 Allied Spotting Procedures for Naval Gunfire Support
2. FMFM 2-7 Fire Support in MAGTF Operations
3. MCRP 3-15.2A Tactical Employment of Mortars
4. MCRP 3-16.1A Tactics, Techniques and Procedures for Field Artillery Target Acquisition
5. MCRP 3-16.6 Multiservice Procedures for the Joint Application of Firepower (J-Fires)
6. MCWP 3-16 Fire Support Coordination in the Ground Combat Element
7. MCWP 3-16.1 Artillery Operations
8. MCWP 3-23.1 Close Air Support
9. MCWP 3-25.3 Marine Air Command and Control System Handbook
10. MCWP 3-40.4 MAGTF Information Operations

SUPPORT REQUIREMENTS:
1. Combined Arms Staff Trainer (CAST)
2. Combat Operations Center Battle Lab

MISCELLANEOUS:

ADMINISTRATIVE INSTRUCTIONS:
1. Live fire is not necessary if adequate computer simulation can be generated.

2. Performance steps are derived from task 0840-FSCC-2105. See Artillery T&R Manual for additional information.

OTI T&R MANUAL

APPENDIX A

FUNCTIONAL AREA MATRIX

1000. FUNCTIONAL AREA MATRIX. The Functional Area Table includes the functional area description.

FUNCTIONAL AREA CODE	DESCRIPTION
PLAN	Planning. Those activities involved with the Marine Corps Planning Process and other staff actions to develop and support a combat Operation Order.
TRNG	Training. Those activities involved with Unit Training Management, conducting unit training, and preparing a unit for combat.
OPS	Operations. Those activities involved with conducting operations to include COC operations, fire support coordination, logistics operations, and all activities pertaining to battle management.

OTI T&R MANUAL

APPENDIX B

TERMS AND DEFINITIONS

Terms in this glossary are subject to change as applicable orders and directives are revised. Terms established by Marine Corps orders or directives take precedence after definitions found in Joint Pub 1-02, *DOD Dictionary of Military and Associated Terms.*

A

After Action Review. A professional discussion of training events conducted after all training to promote learning among training participants. The formality and scope increase with the command level and size of the training evolution. For longer exercises, they should be planned for at predetermined times during an exercise. The results of the AAR shall be recorded on an after action report and forwarded to higher headquarters. The commander and higher headquarters use the results of an AAR to reallocate resources, reprioritize their training plan, and plan for future training.

Assessment. An informal judgment of the unit's proficiency and resources made by a commander or trainer to gain insight into the unit's overall condition. It serves as the basis for the midrange plan. Commanders make frequent use of these determinations during the course of the combat readiness cycle in order to adjust, prioritize or modify training events and plans.

C

Chaining. A process that enables unit leaders to effectively identify subordinate collective events and individual events that support a specific collective event. For example, collective training events at the 4000-level are directly supported by collective events at the 3000-level. Utilizing the building block approach to progressive training, these collective events are further supported by individual training events at the 1000 and 2000-levels. When a higher-level event by its nature requires the completion of lower level events, they are "chained"; Sustainment credit is given for all lower level events chained to a higher event.

Collective Event. A clearly defined, discrete, and measurable activity, action, or event (i.e., task) that requires organized team or unit performance and leads to accomplishment of a mission or function. A collective task is derived from unit missions or higher-level collective tasks. Task accomplishment requires performance of procedures composed of supporting collective or individual tasks. A collective task describes the exact performance a group must perform in the field under actual operational conditions. The term "collective" does not necessarily infer that a unit accomplishes the event. A unit, such as a squad or platoon conducting an attack; may accomplish a collective event or, it may be accomplished by an individual to accomplish a unit mission, such as a battalion supply officer completing a reconciliation of the battalion's CMR. Thus, many collective events will have titles that are the same as individual events; however, the standard and condition will be different because the scope of the collective event is broader.

Collective Training Standards (CTS). Criteria that specify mission and functional area unit proficiency standards for combat, combat support, and combat service support units. They include tasks, conditions, standards, evaluator instruction, and key indicators. CTS are found within collective training events in T&R Manuals.

Combat Readiness Cycle. The combat readiness cycle depicts the relationships within the building block approach to training. The combat readiness cycle progresses from T&R Manual individual core skills training, to the accomplishment of collective training events, and finally, to a unit's participation in a contingency or actual combat. The combat readiness cycle demonstrates the relationship of core capabilities to unit combat readiness. Individual core skills training and the training of collective events lead to unit proficiency and the ability to accomplish the unit's stated mission.

Combat Readiness Percentage (CRP). The CRP is a quantitative numerical value used in calculating collective training readiness based on the E-coded events that support the unit METL. CRP is a concise measure of unit training accomplishments. This numerical value is only a snapshot of training readiness at a specific time. As training is conducted, unit CRP will continuously change.

Component Events. Component events are the major tasks involved in accomplishing a collective event. Listing these tasks guide Marines toward the accomplishment of the event and help evaluators determine if the task has been done to standard. These events may be lower-level collective or individual events that must be accomplished.

Condition. The condition describes the training situation or environment under which the training event or task will take place. Expands on the information in the title by identifying when, where, and why the event or task will occur and what materials, personnel, equipment, environmental provisions, and safety constraints must be present to perform the event or task in a real-world environment. Commanders can modify the conditions of the event to best prepare their Marines to accomplish the assigned mission (e.g. in a desert environment; in a mountain environment; etc.).

Core Competency. Core competency is the comprehensive measure of a unit's ability to accomplish its assigned MET. It serves as the foundation of the T&R Program. Core competencies are those unit core capabilities and individual core skills that support the commander's METL and T/O mission statement. Individual competency is exhibited through demonstration of proficiency in specified core tasks and core plus tasks. Unit proficiency is measured through collective tasks.

Core Capabilities. Core capabilities are the essential functions a unit must be capable of performing during extended contingency/combat operations. Core unit capabilities are based upon mission essential tasks derived from operational plans; doctrine and established tactics; techniques and procedures.

Core Plus Capabilities. Core plus capabilities are advanced capabilities that are environment, mission, or theater specific. Core plus capabilities may entail high-risk, high-cost training for missions that are less likely to be assigned in combat.

Core Plus Skills. Core plus skills are those advanced skills that are environment, mission, rank, or billet specific. 2000-level training is designed to make Marines proficient in core skills in a specific billet or at a specified rank at the Combat Ready level. 3000-8000-level training produces combat leaders and fully qualified section members at the Combat Qualified level. Marines trained at the Combat Qualified level are those the commanding officer feels are capable of accomplishing unit-level missions and of directing the actions of subordinates. Many core plus tasks are learned via MOJT, while others form the base for curriculum in career level MOS courses taught by the formal school.

Core Skills. Core skills are those essential basic skills that "make" a Marine and qualify that Marine for an MOS. They are the 1000-level skills introduced in entry-level training at formal schools and refined in operational units.

D

Defense Readiness Reporting System (DRRS). A comprehensive readiness reporting system that evaluates readiness on the basis of the actual missions and capabilities assigned to the forces. It is a capabilities-based, adaptive, near real-time reporting system for the entire Department of Defense.

Deferred Event. A T&R event that a commanding officer may postpone when in his or her judgment, a lack of logistic support, ammo, ranges, or other training assets requires a temporary exemption. CRP cannot be accrued for deferred "E-Coded" events.

Delinquent Event. An event becomes delinquent when a Marine or unit exceeds the sustainment interval for that particular event. The individual or unit must update the delinquent event by first performing all prerequisite events. When the unit commander deems that performing all prerequisite is unattainable, then the delinquent event will be re-demonstrated under the supervision of the appropriate evaluation authority.

E

E-Coded Event. An "E-Coded" event is a collective T&R event that is a noted indicator of capability or, a noted Collective skill that contributes to the unit's ability to perform the supported MET. As such, only "E-Coded" events are assigned a CRP value and used to calculate a unit's CRP.

Entry-level training. Pipeline training that equips students for service with the Marine Operating Forces.

Evaluation. Evaluation is a continuous process that occurs at all echelons, during every phase of training and can be both formal and informal. Evaluations ensure that Marines and units are capable of conducting their combat mission. Evaluation results are used to reallocate resources, reprioritize the training plan, and plan for future training.

Event (Training). 1) An event is a significant training occurrence that is identified, expanded and used as a building block and potential milestone for a unit's training. An event may include formal evaluations. 2) An event within the T&R Program can be an individual training evolution, a collective training evolution or both. Through T&R events, the unit commander ensures that individual Marines and the unit progress from a combat capable status to a Fully Combat Qualified (FCQ) status.

Event Component. The major procedures (i.e., actions) that must occur to perform a Collective Event to standard.

Exercise Commander (EC). The Commanding General, Marine Expeditionary Force or his appointee will fill this role, unless authority is delegated to the respective commander of the Division, Wing, or FSSG. Responsibilities and functions of the EC include: 1) designate unit(s) to be evaluated, 2) may designate an exercise director, 3) prescribe exercise objectives and T&R events to be evaluated, 4) coordinate with commands or agencies external to the Marine Corps and adjacent Marine Corps commands, when required.

Exercise Director (ED). Designated by the EC to prepare, conduct, and report all evaluation results. Responsibilities and functions of the ED include: 1) Publish a letter of instruction (LOI) that: delineates the T&R events to be evaluated, establishes timeframe of the exercise, lists responsibilities of various elements participating in the exercise, establishes safety requirements/guidelines, and lists coordinating instructions. 2) Designate the TEC and TECG to operate as the central control agency for the exercise. 3) Assign evaluators, to include the senior evaluator, and ensure that those evaluators are properly trained. 4) Develop the general exercise scenario taking into account any objectives/events prescribed by the EC. 5) Arrange for all resources to include: training areas, airspace, aggressor forces, and other required support.

I

Individual Readiness. The individual training readiness of each Marine is measured by the number of individual events required and completed for the rank or billet currently held.

Individual Training. Training that applies to individual Marines. Examples include rifle qualifications and HMMWV driver licensing.

Individual Training Standards (ITS). Specifies training tasks and standards for each MOS or specialty within the Marine Corps. In most cases, once an MOS or community develops a T&R, the ITS order will be cancelled. However, most communities will probably fold a large portion of their ITS into their new T&R manual.

M

Marine Corps Combat Readiness and Evaluation System (MCCRES). An evaluation system designed to provide commanders with a comprehensive set of mission performance standards from which training programs can be developed; and through which the efficiency and effectiveness of training can be evaluated. The Ground T&R Program will eventually replace MCCRES.

Marine Corps Ground Training and Readiness (T&R) Program. The T&R Program is the Marine Corps' primary tool for planning and conducting training, for planning and conducting training evaluation, and for assessing training readiness. The program will provide the commander with standardized programs of instruction for units within the ground combat, combat support, and combat service support communities. It consolidates the ITS, CTS, METL and other individual and unit training management tools. T&R is a program of standards that systematizes commonly accepted skills, is open to innovative change, and above all, tailors the training effort to the unit's mission. Further, T&R serves as a training guide and provides commanders an immediate assessment of unit combat readiness by assigning a CRP to key training events. In short, the T&R Program is a building block approach to training that maximizes flexibility and produces the best-trained Marines possible.

Mission Essential Task(s) MET(s). A MET is a collective task in which an organization must be proficient in order to accomplish an appropriate portion of its wartime mission(s). MET listings are the foundation for the T&R manual; all events in the T&R manual support a MET.

Mission Essential Task List (METL). Descriptive training document that provides units a clear, war fighting focused description of collective actions necessary to achieve wartime mission proficiency. The service-level METL, that which is used as the foundation of the T&R manual, is developed using Marine Corps doctrine, operational plans, T/Os, UJTL, UNTL, and MCTL. For community based T&R manuals, an occupational field METL is developed to focus the community's collective training standards. Commanders develop their unit METL from the service-level METL, operational plans, contingency plans, and SOPs.

Mission Performance Standards (MPS). Criteria that specify mission and functional area unit proficiency standards for combat, combat support and combat service support units. They include tasks, conditions, standards, evaluator instruction, and key indicators. MPS are contained within the MCCRES volumes. The MCCRES volumes are being replaced by T&R Manuals. Collective events will replace MPS.

O

Operational Readiness (DOD, NATO). OR is the capability of a unit/formation, ship, weapon system, or equipment to perform the missions or functions for which it is organized or designed. May be used in a general sense or to express a level or degree of readiness.

P

Performance step. Performance steps are included in the components of an Individual T&R Event. They are the major procedures (i.e., actions) a unit Marine must accomplish to perform an individual event to standard. They describe the procedure the task performer must take to perform the task under operational conditions and provide sufficient information for a task performer to perform the procedure (may necessitate identification of supporting steps, procedures, or actions in outline form). Performance steps follow a logical progression and should be followed sequentially, unless otherwise stated. Normally, performance steps are listed only for 1000-level individual events (those that are taught in the entry-level MOS school). Listing performance steps is optional if the steps are already specified in a published reference.

Prerequisite Event. Prerequisites are the academic training and/or T&R events that must be completed prior to attempting the event.

R

Readiness (DOD). Readiness is the ability of U.S. military forces to fight and meet the demands of the national military strategy. Readiness is the synthesis of two distinct but interrelated levels: a) Unit readiness--The ability to provide capabilities required by combatant commanders to execute assigned missions. This is derived from the ability of each unit to deliver the outputs for which it was designed. b) Joint readiness--The combatant commander's ability to integrate and synchronize ready combat and support forces to execute assigned missions.

S

Section Skill Tasks. Section skills are those competencies directly related to unit functioning. They are group rather than individual in nature, and require participation by a section (S-1, S-2, S-3, etc).

Simulation Training. Simulators provide the additional capability to develop and hone core and core plus skills. Accordingly, the development of simulator training events for appropriate T&R syllabi can help maintain valuable combat resources while reducing training time and cost. Therefore, in cases where simulator fidelity and capabilities are such that simulator training closely matches that of actual training events, T&R Manual developers may include the option of using simulators to accomplish the training. CRP credit will be earned for E-coded simulator events based on assessment of relative training event performance.

Standard. A standard is a statement that establishes criteria for how well a task or learning objective must be performed. The standard specifies how well, completely, or accurately a process must be performed or product produced. For higher-level collective events, it describes why the event is being done and the desired end-state of the event. Standards become more specific for lower-level events and outline the accuracy, time limits, sequencing, quality, product, process, restrictions, etc., that indicate the minimum acceptable level of performance required of the event. At a minimum, both collective and individual training standards consist of a task, the condition under which the task is to be performed, and the evaluation criteria that will be used to verify that the task has been performed to a satisfactory level.

Sustainment Training. Periodic retraining or demonstration of an event required maintaining the minimum acceptable level of proficiency or capability required to accomplish a training objective. Sustainment training goes beyond the entry-level and is designed to maintain or further develop proficiency in a given set of skills.

Systems Approach to Training (SAT). An orderly process for analyzing, designing, developing, implementing, and evaluating a unit's training program to ensure the unit, and the Marines of that unit acquire the knowledge and skills essential for the successful conduct of the unit's wartime missions.

T

Training Task. This describes a direct training activity that pertains to an individual Marine. A task is composed of 3 major components: a description of what is to be done, a condition, and a standard.

Technical Exercise Controller (TEC). The TEC is appointed by the ED, and usually comes from his staff or a subordinate command. The TEC is the senior evaluator within the TECG and should be of equal or higher grade than the commander(s) of the unit(s) being evaluated. The TEC is responsible for ensuring that the evaluation is conducted following the instructions contained in this order and MCO 1553.3A. Specific T&R manuals are used as the source for evaluation criteria.

Tactical Exercise Control Group (TECG). A TECG is formed to provide subject matter experts in the functional areas being evaluated. The benefit of establishing a permanent TECG is to have resident, dedicated evaluation authority experience, and knowledgeable in evaluation technique. The responsibilities and functions of the TECG include: 1) developing a detailed exercise scenario to include the objectives and events prescribed by the EC/ED in the exercise LOI; 2) conducting detailed evaluator training prior to the exercise; 3) coordinating and controlling role players and aggressors; 4) compiling the evaluation data submitted by the evaluators and submitting required results to the ED; 5) preparing and conducting a detailed exercise debrief for the evaluated unit(s).

Training Plan. Training document that outlines the general plan for the conduct of individual and collective training in an organization for specified periods of time.

U

Unit CRP. Unit CRP is a percentage of the E-coded collective events that support the unit METL accomplished by the unit. Unit CRP is the average of all MET CRP.

Unit Evaluation. All units in the Marine Corps must be evaluated, either formally or informally, to ensure they are capable of conducting their combat mission. Informal evaluations should take place during all training events. The timing of formal evaluations is critical and should, when appropriate, be directly related to the units' operational deployment cycle. Formal evaluations should take place after the unit has been staffed with the majority of its personnel, has had sufficient time to train to individual and collective standards, and early enough in the training cycle so there is sufficient time to correctly identified weaknesses prior to deployment. All combat units and units' task organized for combat require formal evaluations prior to operational deployments.

Unit Training Management (UTM). Unit training management is the use of the SAT and Marine Corps training principles in a manner that maximizes training results and focuses the training priorities of the unit on its wartime mission. UTM governs the major peacetime training activity of the Marine Corps and applies to all echelons of the Total Force.

W

Waived Event. An event that is waived by a commanding officer when in his or her judgment, previous experience or related performance satisfies the requirement of a particular event.